KV-370-874

Table of Contents

Tables

Diagrams

BASIC STATISTICS OF IRELAND

THE LAND

Area (thousand sq. km)	70	Population of major cities, 1986	
Agricultural area, 1989, as per cent		census (thousands)	
of total area	80	Dublin (County and Co. Borough)	1 021
		Cork, Co. Borough	133
		Limerick, Co. Borough	56

THE PEOPLE

Population (April 1990)	3 503 000	Net emigration:	
No. of inhabitants per sq. km	50	Annual average 1981–1990	20 600
Increase in population: annual		Annual average per thousand of population	5.9
average 1981–1990	10 200	Labour force, total, April 1990	1 303 000
Natural increase in population:		Civilian employment in:	
annual average 1981–1990	30 700	Agriculture, forestry and fishing	165 000
		Industry and construction	322 000
		Other sectors	633 000

THE GOVERNMENT

Public current expenditure on goods		Composition of Parliament (June 1989):	
and services, 1989 (as per cent of GNP)	18		seats
General government current revenue, 1989		Fianna Fail	77
(as per cent of GNP)	50	Fine Gael	55
Public debt, 31st December 1989		Labour	15
(as cent of GNP)	119	Workers Party	7
		Progressive Democrats	6
		Others	6
		Last general election: June 1989	

FOREIGN TRADE

Exports:		Imports:	
Exports of goods and services, as per		Imports of goods and services, as per	
cent of GNP (1989)	77	cent of GNP (1989)	66
Main exports, 1989 (per cent of total):		Main imports, 1989 (per cent of total):	
Machinery and electrical goods	32	Machinery and electrical goods	38
of which:		Petroleum, petroleum products and	
Office machinery and data processing		related materials	4
equipment	20	Textile manufactures	3
Meat and meat preparations	6	Iron and steel	2
Dairy products and birds' eggs	5	Clothing and footwear	5
Textile manufactures	2	Main suppliers, 1989 (per cent of total):	
Live animals chiefly for food	1	United Kingdom	41
Clothing and footwear	2	Other European Economic Community	25
Beverages	2	United States	16
Organic chemicals	6		
Medicinal and pharmaceutical products	3		
Main customers, 1989 (per cent of total):			
United Kingdom	34		
Other European Economic Community	41		
United States	8		

THE CURRENCY

Monetary unit: Irish pound		Currency unit per US dollar,	
		average of daily figures:	
		Year 1990	0.60
		March 1991	0.60

Note: An international comparison of certain basic statistics is given in an annex table.

This Survey is based on the Secretariat's study prepared for the annual review of Ireland by the Economic and Development Review Committee on 6th March 1991.

●

After revisions in the light of discussions during the review, final approval of the Survey for publication was given by the Committee on 18th March 1991.

●

The previous Survey of Ireland was issued in July 1989.

Introduction

The remarkable improvement in Irish economic performance noted in the previous *OECD Economic Survey of Ireland* continued in 1989 and 1990, helped by a favourable external environment. The policy commitments made in the *Programme for National Recovery,* to maintain the value of the Irish pound within the EMS, to moderate pay increases, and to reduce the national debt/GNP ratio by curtailing the public sector borrowing requirement have been carried through, with markedly beneficial effects on interest rates and business confidence. Investment has recovered strongly, and as a result of productivity gains and wage moderation, profitability and international competitiveness have improved. GNP has grown by an average of just under 5 per cent a year over the last two years, while the rate of inflation had fallen to below 3 per cent by the end of 1990. This good performance owes much to the broadly-based consensus which has allowed macroeconomic policies to focus on the medium term, emphasising continuity and consistency rather than short-term activism. It has also owed a great deal to a favourable world trading environment, in which rising export demand, buoyant tax revenues and lower real interest rates have made the goal of reducing government and external imbalances easier to attain. The pace of private sector job creation has increased considerably. However, the unemployment rate, though significantly reduced, remains well above the European average.

The economy is now entering a critical stage in which the pace of the expansion has begun to slacken, and the stimulus provided by external factors has started to weaken. Ireland's major trading partner, the United Kingdom, and the United States, are in recession, while increased demand for credit to finance eastern European – particularly East German – reconstruction has put upward pressure on real interest rates in Europe. Prospects for agriculture are being affected by budgetary constraints within the EC and trade pressures within the GATT. With the public debt/GNP ratio still at 111 per cent, fiscal policy needs to stay restrictive. GNP growth could be halved compared with

9

1990, and while inflation may decline further the unemployment rate is likely to remain high. Consolidating the fiscal gains made in the 1987-90 period may thus prove difficult. It will require a continued medium-term commitment to the macroeconomic policies followed in the last four years. The recently agreed *Programme for Economic and Social Progress* indicates a renewed commitment in this respect. However, structural impediments continue to hamper economic development, competitiveness and efficiency. Accordingly, additional structural reform is necessary especially with respect to the tax and benefit systems.

Following a discussion of short-term trends and prospects in Part I, monetary and fiscal policies are analysed in Part II, including the requirements for a further reduction in the public debt burden. Part III analyses medium-term prospects and policy issues. Part IV contains a special study of tax reform. Conclusions are presented in Part V.

I. Recent trends and short-term prospects

The recovery in perspective

Output and Employment

The major indicators of economic performance show an across-the-board improvement in the last four years, although the major driving forces have altered as the expansion has matured *(Diagram 1)*. In the early years of the recovery, growth was led by a strong increase in export production, reflecting the pick-up in world trade: there was a clear divergence between net exports and domestic demand growth. Since 1989, economic growth has also been supported by a strong expansion in business-fixed investment, as the improved business climate generated the demand for greater industrial capacity. The sharp rise in capital spending since 1987 contrasts with the virtually decade-long decline in the investment/GNP ratio which preceded it *(Diagram 2)*. Manufacturing output has recovered strongly, underpinned both by strong growth of export markets and improving Irish cost competitiveness. High technology sectors have grown particularly fast. Total industrial production is estimated to have grown by close to 12 per cent in 1989 and by around 7 per cent in 1990. Gross agricultural product has grown more erratically, declining by around 1 per cent in volume terms in 1989 due to unfavourable weather conditions but increasing by over 10 per cent in 1990. The output of the services sector has grown more modestly, averaging about 2 per cent a year.

Total employment grew by about 13 000 jobs a year on average between 1987 and 1990 (about 1¼ per cent a year) *(Table 1 and Diagram 2)*. Private sector employment in non-agricultural activities has been expanding significantly faster, since the total employment figure is affected by a decline in public sector employment and the trend decrease in the number of agricultural workers[1]. At the same time, the labour force has declined, because of net emigration. Following a decade of net inflows in the 1970s, net emigration

Diagram 1. **MACROECONOMIC PERFORMANCE**

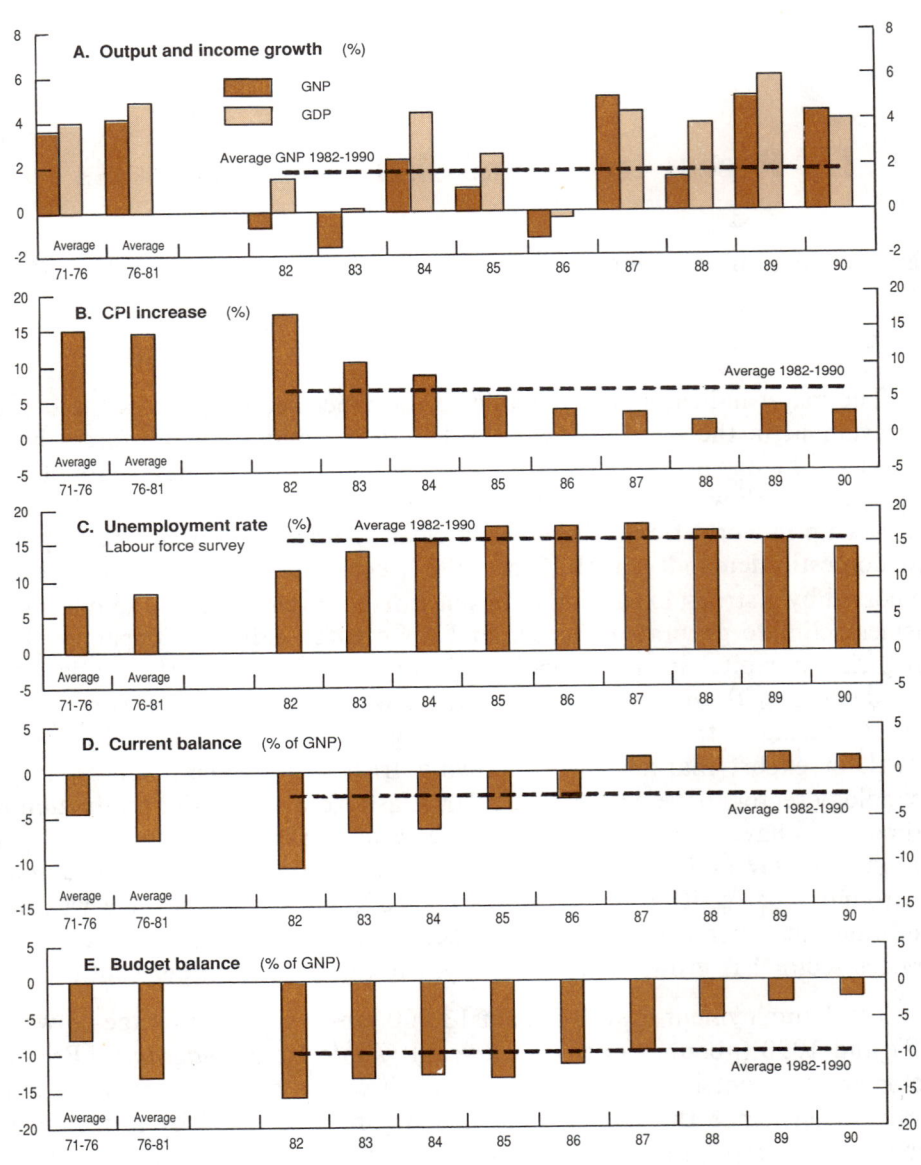

A. Output and income growth (%)

GNP

GDP

Average GNP 1982-1990

B. CPI increase (%)

Average 1982-1990

C. Unemployment rate (%) Average 1982-1990
Labour force survey

D. Current balance (% of GNP)

Average 1982-1990

E. Budget balance (% of GNP)

Average 1982-1990

Sources: Department of Finance, *Budget 1989* and OECD Secretariat.

Diagram 2. **CYCLICAL INDICATORS**

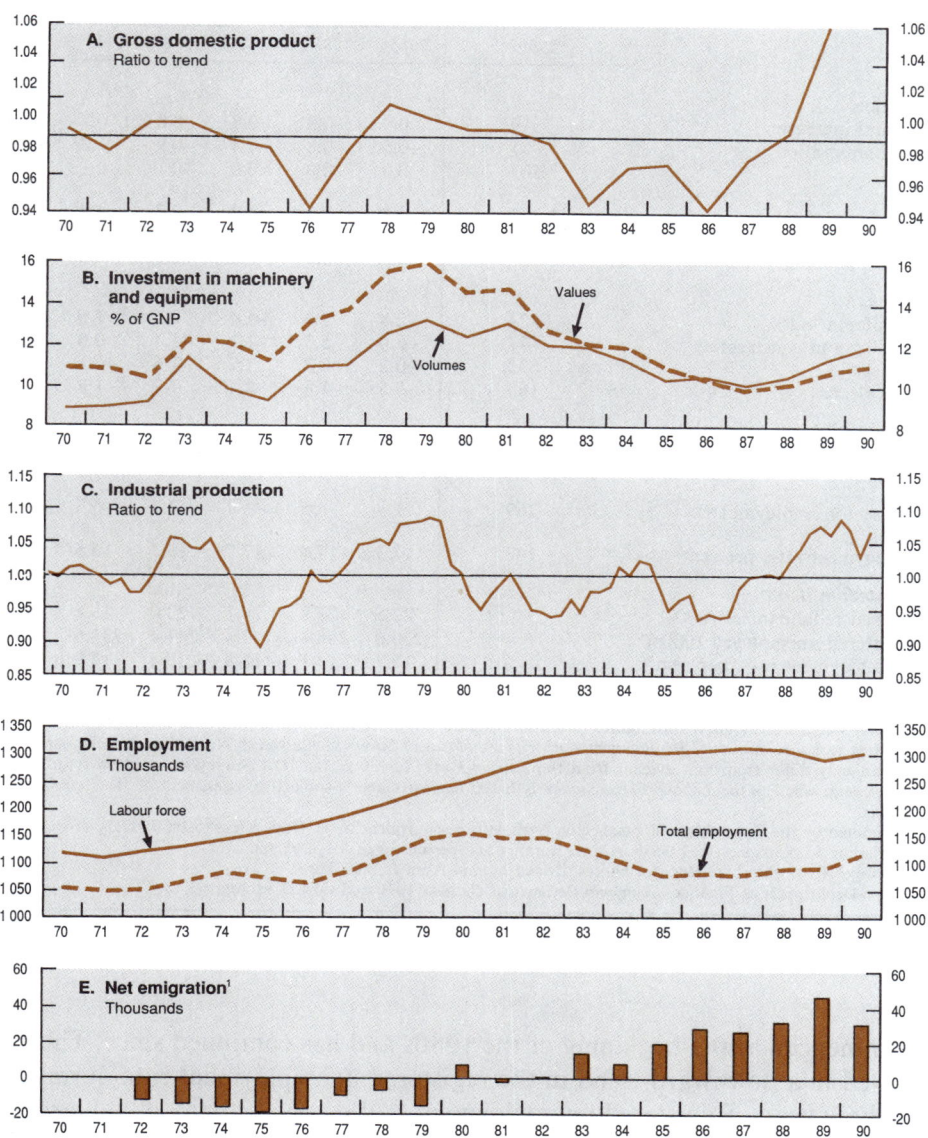

A. Gross domestic product
Ratio to trend

B. Investment in machinery and equipment
% of GNP

Values

Volumes

C. Industrial production
Ratio to trend

D. Employment
Thousands

Labour force

Total employment

E. Net emigration[1]
Thousands

1. Data refer to total emigration, not emigration from the labour force.
Source: OECD.

13

Table 1. **Labour market developments**

	Memorandum item: Number (000s)	Annual percentage growth rates					
	1990	1985	1986	1987	1988	1989	1990
Population[1]							
Natural increase	19	0.9	0.8	0.8	0.8	0.7	0.5
Net immigration	−31	−0.6	−0.8	−0.8	−0.9	−1.3	−0.9
Total	3 503	0.3	0.0	0.0	−0.1	−0.1	−0.3
Labour force[2]	**1 303**	**−0.2**	**0.2**	**0.3**	**−0.2**	**−1.4**	**0.9**
Total employment[2]	**1 120**	**−2.2**	**0.2**	**−0.1**	**1.0**	**0.0**	**2.8**
Of which:							
Manufacturing	224	−2.8	2.9	−1.4	0.5	1.0	4.2
Building and construction	77	−8.4	−5.3	−1.4	−1.4	0.0	10.0
Services	633	−0.2	0.7	1.7	1.6	−0.1	1.9
Agriculture	165	−5.5	−1.8	−2.4	1.2	−1.8	1.2
Manufacturing, by nationality[3]							
Irish		−3.5	−3.3	−4.0	−0.6	2.0	0.0
Foreign		−2.3	−0.4	−1.9	2.6	1.9	2.5
Public sector employment[4]	269	−1.5	−0.6	−1.7	−3.3	−5.5	−0.4
Unemployment rate, per cent[2]	**183**	**17.3**	**17.4**	**17.7**	**16.7**	**15.6**	**14.0**
Memorandum items:							
Notified redundancies (000s)		22.5	22.8	24.1	23.0	13.4	13.3
Registered unemployed (000s)[5]		230.6	236.4	247.4	241.4	231.6	224.7
Unemployment rate, per cent[6]		17.7	18.1	18.8	18.4	17.9	17.2

1. Estimated; net migration is calculated as a residual.
2. Labour Force Survey, mid-April figures (see also Diagram 1).
3. Figures based on *Industrial Development Authority Employment Survey* conducted in November of each year. Trend shown may differ from that evident from the *Labour Force Survey* as the IDA Survey is based on returns from employers, whereas the *Labour Force Survey* is based on respondent's subjective assessment of their employment status.
4. Estimated by the Department of Finance on a whole time equivalent basis. Data refers to 1st January of each year.
5. Excluding workers on systemtic short-time working and persons aged 65 years and over.
6. Average of monthly Live Register figures divided by mid-April Labour Force.
Sources: Department of Finance, *Economic Review and Outlook* 1990 and OECD Secretariat.

recommenced at the beginning of the 1980s and has continued since. This has resulted in a downward trend in the registered unemployment rate during the last three years. Registered unemployment had reached a peak of a quarter of a million in May 1987, corresponding to an unemployment rate of 19 per cent *(Table 1)*. In 1989 the average number of unemployed fell by almost 10 000 (4 per cent) and the unemployment rate to 18 per cent. The decline in the unemployment rate continued into 1990, despite slowing emigration, due to weakening labour demand in the United Kingdom. After reaching a peak in the twelve months to April 1989, the net outflow is estimated to have subsequently fallen substantially.

Productivity, profitability and inflation

Labour productivity, measured by growth of GDP per employed person, showed an annual average gain of 3½ per cent from 1986 to 1989 *(Diagram 3).*Productivity in manufacturing industry rose by an average of 12 per cent a year over the same period, before slowing down somewhat in 1990. At the same time, there has been a general adherence to the wage restraint agreed to in the *Programme for National Recovery (PNR),* both in the public and private sectors. An improved industrial relations climate has been reflected in a considerable reduction in the number of work days lost due to strikes, and in wage settlements which have lagged productivity gains. Unit labour costs in manufacturing have fallen substantially, since the rate of increase in average hourly earnings in manufacturing fell from 7 to 4 per cent a year between 1986 and 1989. Total economy unit labour costs have grown by only 2 per cent a year over the same four-year period. The GNP deflator has risen by just over 4 per cent a year on average, so that the share of profits in business sector value added has risen substantially *(Diagram 3, panel B)*[2]. This trend has been largely due to a significant rise in the share of profits in manufacturing.

The diminishing contribution of unit wage costs to price changes is evident from Diagram 4. At the same time, there has been a trend decrease in the contribution of indirect taxes to price rises, reflecting a decline in indirect tax rates (a trend which is expected to continue with the process of tax harmonisation within the EC). The consumer price index has also fluctuated with changes in the terms of trade, though by less than was formerly the case. The CPI rose by 4 per cent in 1989, but by 2¾ per cent (year-on-year) up to November 1990, as the strength of the Irish pound brought gains in the terms of trade *(Table 2).*With the inflation differential *vis-à-vis* Germany being eliminated by the end of 1990, the inflation rate is now significantly below that of the United Kingdom. As a result of appreciation against the dollar, the increase in overall prices due to the rise in the dollar price of oil in the second half of 1990 has not been severe. The Irish economy is in any case much less

15

_Diagram 3. **UNIT LABOUR COSTS AND PROFIT SHARE**

A. Unit labour costs and their determinants, total economy
Annual per cent growth

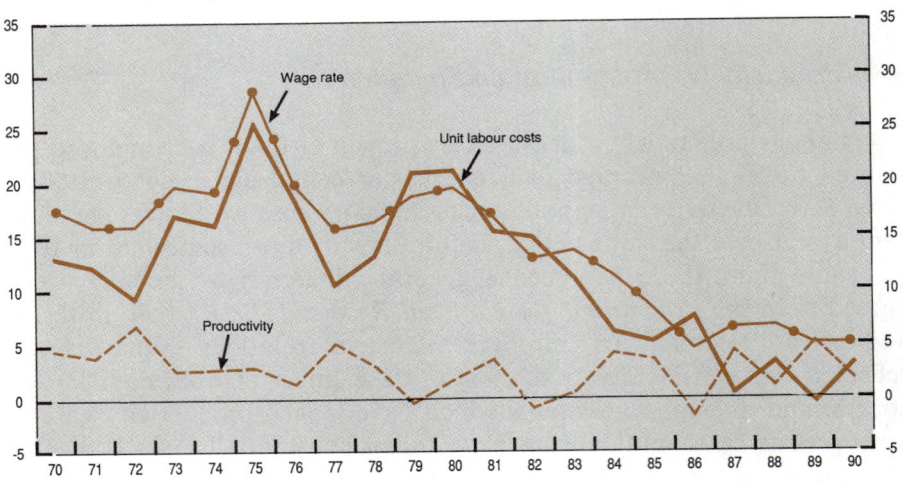

B. Non-wage share[1]
Per cent

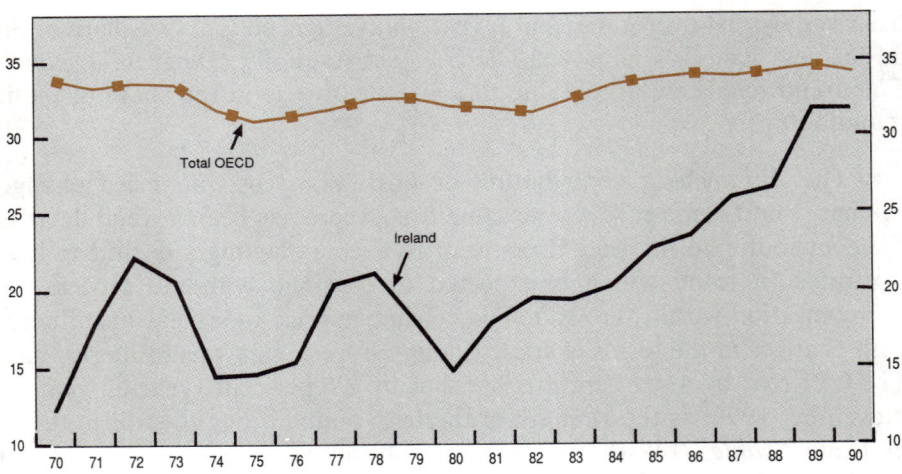

1. Share of the non-wage component in net output of business sector.
Source: OECD, *Economic Outlook.*

16

Diagram 4. **INFLATION AND ITS PROXIMATE CAUSES**

A. Comparative consumer price increases Change over 12 months

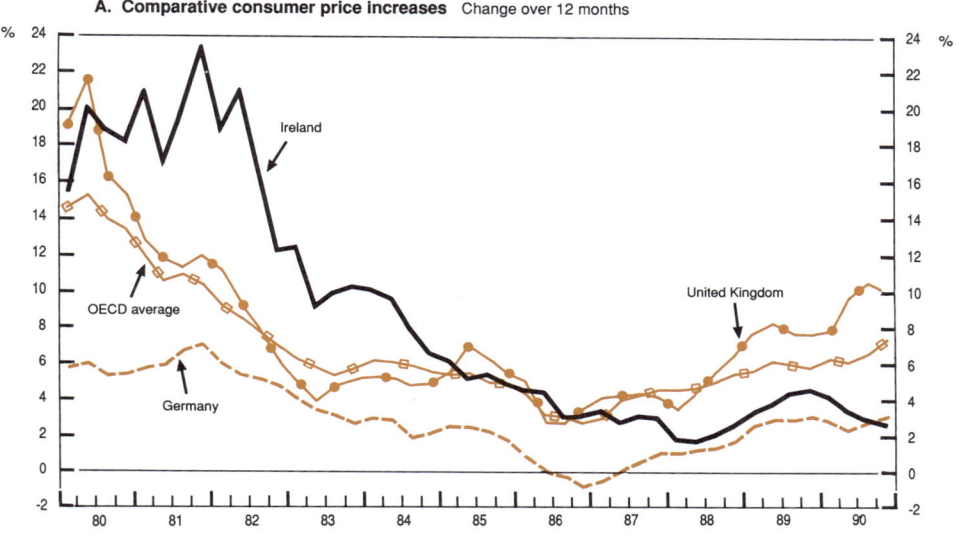

B. Contributions to price changes[1]

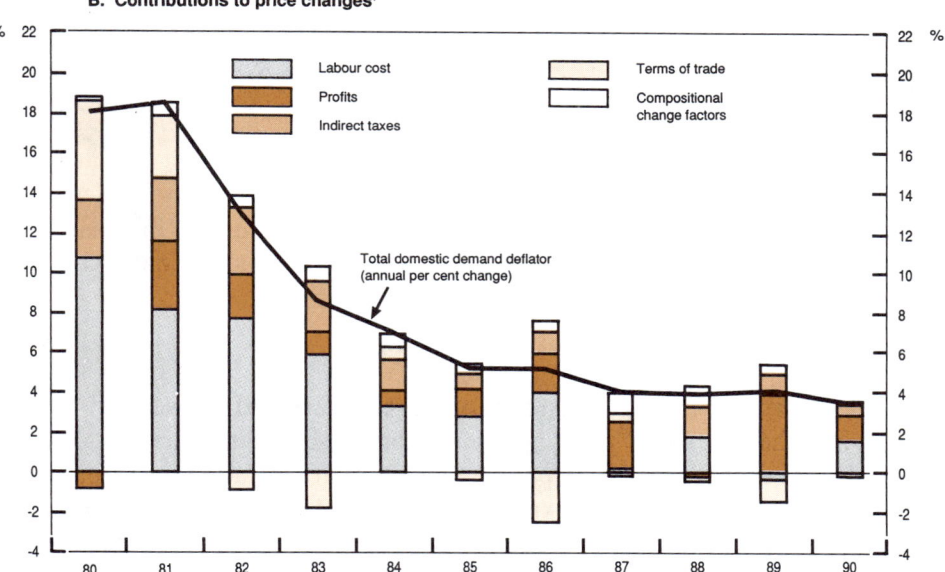

1. See technical annex for a detailed explanation.
Sources: OECD, *Main Economic Indicators;* Secretariat estimates.

Table 2. **Prices, wages and non-wage incomes**

Percentage changes over preceding period (annual rates)

	1985	1986	1987	1988	1989	1990
Consumer prices						
All items	5.4	3.8	‑3.2	2.1	4.0	3.4
Food	3.9	4.4	2.7	2.9	4.7	1.7
Energy	7.3	−6.4	−1.6	−0.6	4.3	2.6
Wholesale prices						
Manufacturing[1]	3.9	0.0	2.5	4.1	4.8	−1.6
Agriculture[2]	−2.7	−0.5	4.0	10.5	5.0	−7.9[3]
Wages[4]	11.5	7.2	4.9	4.3	4.0	4.1[3]
Non-wage incomes						
Non-agricultural sector[5]	16.1	8.8	10.2	11.0	14.7	..
Total business sector[6]	22.6	23.6	25.9	26.6	31.7	31.7
Memorandum items:						
Real wages[7]	1.7	3.2	1.6	2.2	−0.3	0.7
Terms of trade	0.4	4.3	0.1	0.6	0.1	−2.7[8]

1. Price index of manufacturing industry output.
2. Price index of total agricultural output.
3. Average of the first three quarters of 1990.
4. Hourly earnings in manufacturing.
5. Trading profits and other professional earnings in the non-agricultural sector.
6. Share of the non-wage component in net output of the business sector. OECD calculations.
7. Hourly earnings in manufacturing deflated by the consumer price index (all items).
8. First 11 months of 1990 compared to same period of 1989.
Sources: CSO, *Economic Series; National Income and Exependiture,* OECD Secretariat.

dependent on oil now than it was at the end of the 1970s, due to increased fuel efficiency and rising domestic output of energy from off-shore natural gas.

Private sector demand

The volume of private consumption barely increased between 1979 and 1986, while the volume of public consumption of goods and services grew by almost 10 per cent. Since 1986, public consumption has fallen by 12 per cent, while private consumption has expanded by about 13½ per cent, or over 3 per cent per year on average *(Table 3).*Personal spending rose rather modestly in the first two years of the recovery, but began to expand more rapidly in 1989, reaching 5¼ per cent and becoming more broadly-based as the expansion progressed. Increased disposable income, greater consumer confidence and

Table 3. **Demand and output**

Percentage volume changes, 1985 prices, annual rates

	1987 current price, Ir£ million	1980-86 average	1987	1988	1989	1990[1]
Private consumption	11 783	0.4	2.2	2.5	5.2	3.1
Public consumption	3 577	1.3	−4.9	−4.2	−3.5	0.0
Gross fixed investment	3 338	−2.9	−3.7	2.6	12.0	9.5
Of which:						
Building and construction	1 687	−3.3	−8.3	−0.7	9.8	8.9
Machinery and equipment	1 651	−2.5	1.1	5.7	14.0	10.1
Final domestic demand	18 697	−0.1	−0.3	1.2	4.9	3.9
Stockbuilding[2]	27	0.4	−0.7	−0.9	1.1	2.3
Total domestic demand	**18 724**	**0.2**	**−0.9**	**0.4**	**6.0**	**6.0**
Exports	11 785	7.2	13.4	8.7	10.1	4.9
Imports	10 468	3.6	5.0	3.9	10.9	7.8
Net factor income paid abroad[2]	1 957	−1.8	0.1	−2.9	−1.8	−0.3
Foreign balance[2]	**−640**	**0.2**	**6.0**	**1.0**	**−1.3**	**−2.0**
GNP (market prices)	**18 084**	**0.4**	**5.0**	**1.4**	**5.0**	**4.4**
Memorandum items:						
GDP (market prices)	20 041	1.9	4.4	3.9	5.9	4.0
GDP (factor cost)	17 933	1.9	4.5	5.2	5.5	..
Of which:						
Agriculture	1 925	1.8	6.0	4.8	−1.2	..
Industry	6 568	3.0	7.2	9.2	11.7	..
Distribution, transport and communication	3 162	−0.3	2.5	6.7	4.0	..
Public administration and defence	1 190	1.3	−2.5	−5.5	−2.9	..
Gross national disposable income[3]	18 976	1.0	3.9	1.9	5.2	..

1. OECD estimates.
2. Contribution to GNP growth.
3. GNP plus net current international transfers with terms-of-trade adjustment included (transfers are deflated by the implicit import deflator, and the average of the expenditure and output-based estimates for GNP has been used).
Sources: CSO *National Income and Expenditure*; OECD Secretariat.

falling interest rates meant that demand spread from purchases of new cars to replace ageing stock to a broader range of durable goods, including electrical goods. Consumer borrowing increased substantially in 1989 and the saving ratio fell, as the "wealth effect" of lower interest rates was reflected in higher

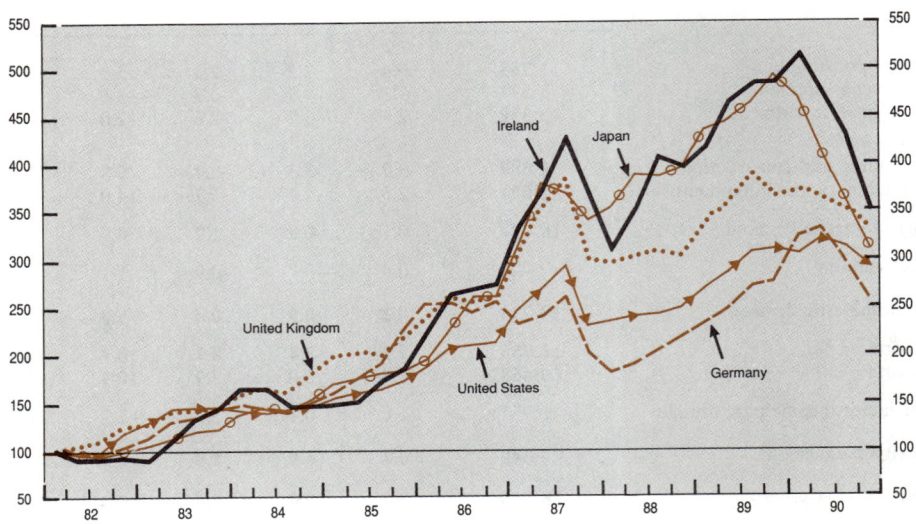

Diagram 5. **SHARE PRICE MOVEMENTS**
Q1 1982 = 100

Source: OECD *Main Economic Indicators.*

asset values. Tax cuts have also helped to increase the disposable income of households. For most of the 1980s taxes on personal income increased at a faster pace than personal income itself, but since 1988 the ratio of tax to personal income has fallen slightly. Signs that the rapid pace of consumption growth was unsustainable began to appear from mid-1990. Although consumer spending for the year as a whole was up about 3 per cent in real terms in 1990, most of the increase occurred in the first part of the year. Higher interest rates, a 30 per cent fall in stock prices *(Diagram 5),* declining farm incomes and the Gulf crisis were probably the major factors behind the slowdown.

Private fixed capital formation, which, as noted, has become one of the driving forces of the expansion, has been rising rapidly on a broad basis since 1989. Private residential investment has been extremely buoyant, supported

20

by declining mortgage rates up to the spring of 1989. Industrial and commercial building and construction have also risen substantially, as has investment in machinery and equipment. Imports of capital goods are estimated to have risen by over 26 per cent in volume terms in 1989 alone. Following a period of steady decline since 1984, during which the share of public investment in total gross capital formation fell from almost 50 to 32 per cent, public infrastructure investment has been boosted since 1988, helped by EC funding under the Community Support Framework.

The external sector

The pattern of demand growth has been distorted by stockbuilding of agricultural export produce. Agricultural exports were buoyant until 1990, when they began to be affected by weak demand in Europe and the closure of certain middle eastern markets. Following a modest rise in stocks of both agricultural and manufacturing products in 1989, heavy involuntary stockbuilding occurred in 1990, associated with a substantial increase in EC intervention stocks for agricultural products. As a result, total domestic demand is shown as growing by about 6 per cent in volume terms in 1990, compared with GDP growth of 4 per cent. Much of the growth contribution from stockbuilding had as a counterpart a decline in real net exports, which implied a substantially negative contribution to demand growth from the external sector in 1990.

As a result of comparatively modest increases in real wage rates, Ireland's competitive position, as measured by movements in relative unit labour costs in manufacturing in a common currency, has strengthened in recent years *(Diagram 6, panel B)*[3]. This has been reflected in an improvement in Irish manufacturing export performance, as the growth of export volumes has exceeded export market growth *(Diagram 7)*. Trade has tended to diversify away from the United Kingdom towards other EC countries and the United States *(Annex Table A2)*. Although the United Kingdom is still by far Ireland's largest trading partner, its share in both Irish exports and non-oil imports declined to one-third in 1989 from about one-half in the 1970s.

Reflecting the strength of domestic demand, import volumes have also grown rapidly in the last two years. In addition to buoyant imports of consumer goods, those of capital goods and parts and semi-processed goods were also strong, mirroring the export expansion of the manufacturing industry. As

21

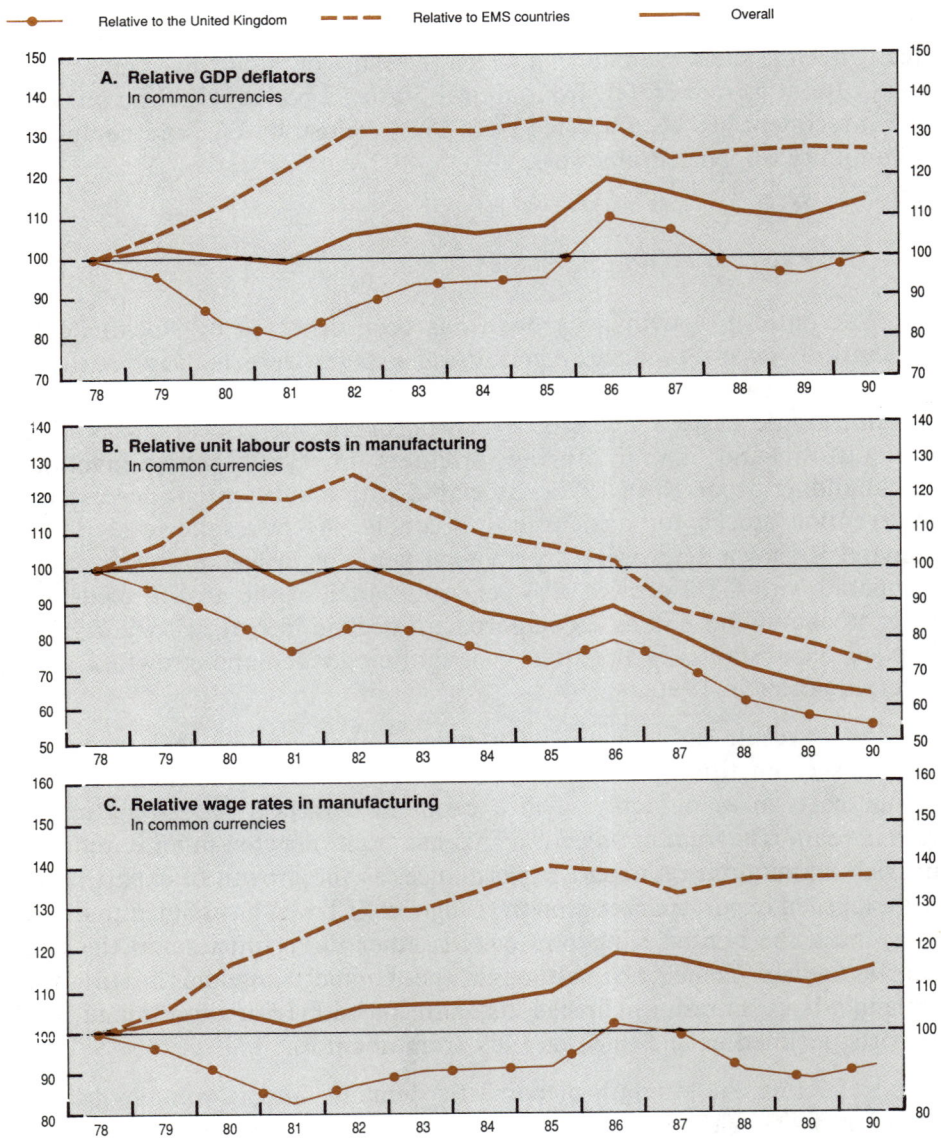

Diagram 6. **MEASURES OF COMPETITIVENESS**[1]
1978 = 100

Relative to the United Kingdom ——— Relative to EMS countries – – – Overall ———

A. Relative GDP deflators
In common currencies

B. Relative unit labour costs in manufacturing
In common currencies

C. Relative wage rates in manufacturing
In common currencies

1. Relative to trade weighted average of trading partners.
Source: OECD.

22

a result, the trade surplus stabilised at around 10 per cent of GNP in both 1989 and 1990, following several years of rapid improvement. Non-agricultural trade is in virtual balance, so that the trade surplus is almost wholly

Diagram 7. **EXPORT PERFORMANCE**
1985 = 100

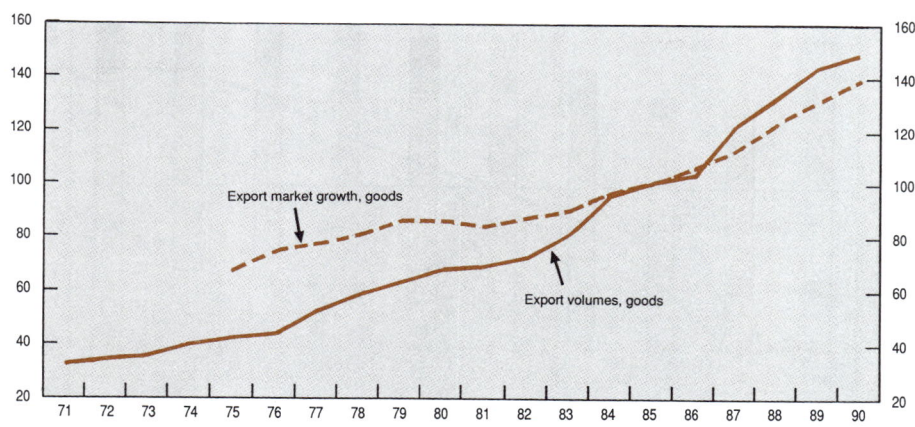

Source: OECD.

accounted for by trade in agricultural products *(Diagrams 8 and 9).*The explanation for the turnaround in the trade balance during the 1980s is to be found in the manufacturing sector, however. The expansion of highly capital-intensive and export-oriented foreign enterprises has resulted in an increasing surplus in high-tech trade[4], although strong export growth in domestically-owned, labour-intensive industries has also contributed to a declining deficit in that sector in recent years *(Table 4 and Diagram 8).*

The deficit in net factor income flows widened further to nearly 15 per cent of GDP in 1989, due to increasing profit repatriation and the rise in debt interest payments abroad, especially by semi-state and private institutions

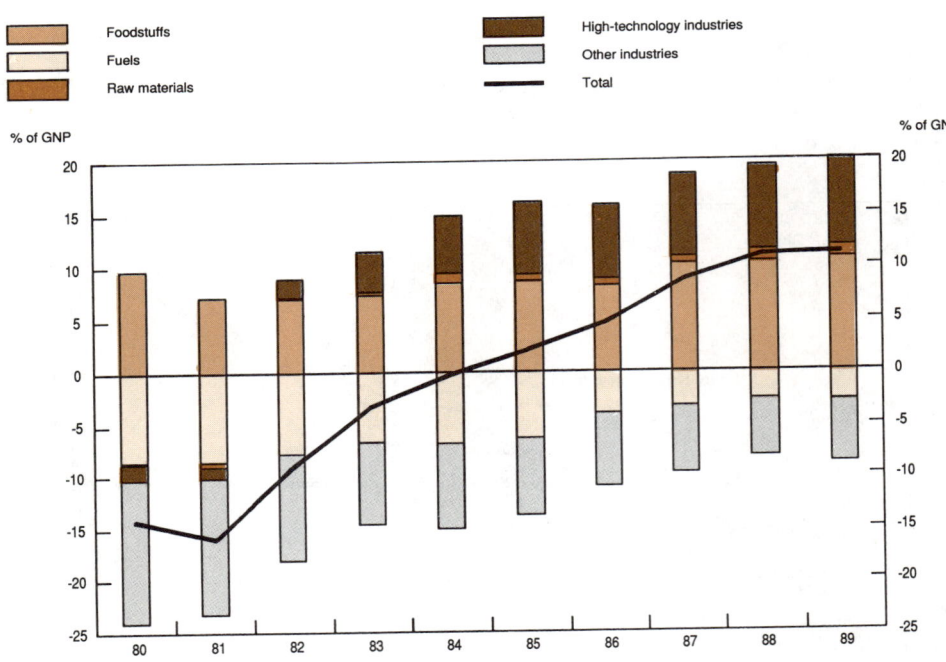

Diagram 8. **COMMODITY COMPOSITION OF NET GOODS EXPORTS**

Customs basis

Foodstuffs

Fuels

Raw materials

High-technology industries

Other industries

Total

% of GNP

% of GN

Source: OECD, *Foreign Trade Statistics.*

(Diagram 10 and Table 5). The increase in profit outflows has been the counterpart of the strong export performance of foreign-owned firms. The remainder of the external services account returned to surplus in 1989 mainly due to a rise in net revenues from tourism. Transfer receipts continued to grow in 1990 as a result of increased receipts from EC funds, but all in all the invisibles deficit widened further in 1989. As a result, the current-account surplus declined by half a percentage point to 1¾ per cent of GNP. This appears to have been reversed in 1990, when a ¾ per cent increase seems to have occurred.

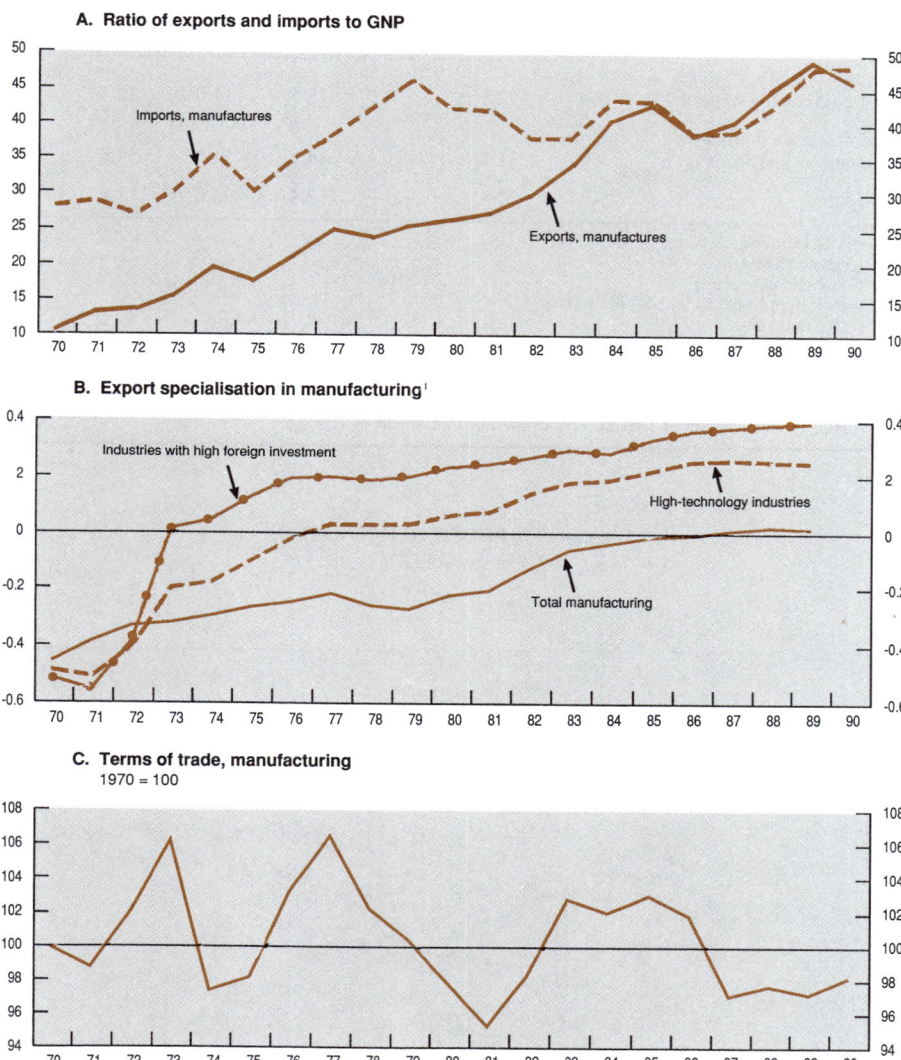

Diagram 9. **DEVELOPMENT OF MANUFACTURING TRADE**

A. Ratio of exports and imports to GNP

Imports, manufactures

Exports, manufactures

B. Export specialisation in manufacturing[1]

Industries with high foreign investment

High-technology industries

Total manufacturing

C. Terms of trade, manufacturing
1970 = 100

1. (Exports - imports)/(exports + imports). For definitions of high-technology industries, see footnote 1, Table 4. Industries with high foreign investment are SITC divisions 51, 54, 75, 87, 88.
Source: OECD.

Table 4. Growth in manufacturing exports

Per cent change, at annual rate, value terms

	Weight in total (1990)	1980-85	1986	1987	1988	1989	1990
Total manufacturing exports	100	22.8	−3.0	13.5	17.0	21.7	1.0
Exports of sectors dominated by foreign-owned firms[1]	58	31.8	−4.1	14.2	11.6	24.8	0.5
Other exports	42	13.9	−1.3	12.4	25.0	17.6	1.8

1. Includes SITC divisions:
    51 (organic chemicals)
    52 (inorganic chemicals)
    54 (medical and pharmaceutical products)
    75 (office machines)
    76 (telecommunications)
    77 (electrical machinery, apparatus and appliances)
    87 (professional, scienfitic and controlling apparatus)
    88 (photographic apparatus, optical goods, watches and clocks)
Source: CSO, *Trade Statistics of Ireland,* various issues, Department of Finance.

Diagram 10. **PROFIT REPATRIATION**
Per cent of GDP

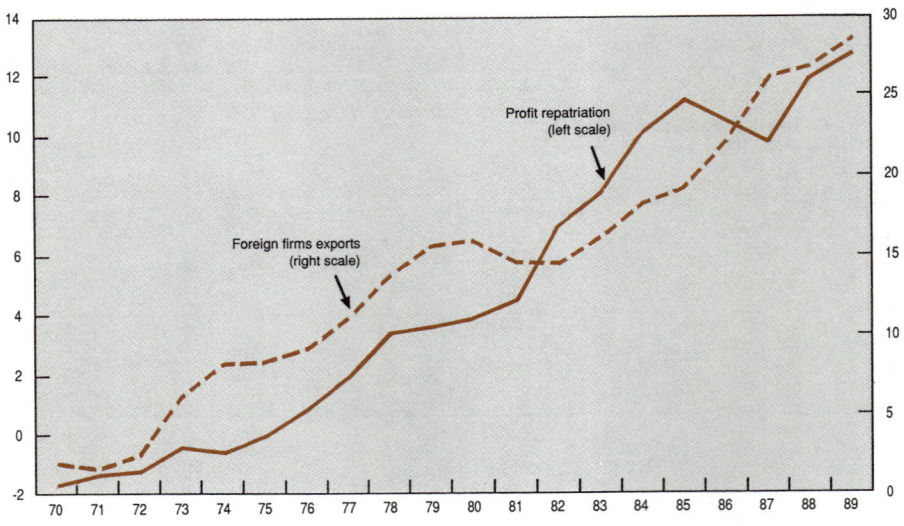

Source: OECD, *Economic Outlook, Trade by Commodities,* Series B.

26

Table 5. Current account of the balance of payments[1]

Ir£ million

	1985	1986	1987	1988	1989	1990
Exports, f.o.b.	9 527	9 181	10 447	12 073	14 358	14 492
Imports, c.i.f.	9 390	8 746	9 137	10 048	12 114	12 681
Trade balance	**137**	**435**	**1 310**	**2 025**	**2 244**	**1 811**
Tourism, net[2]	283	138	175	212	285	..
Other services, net	−78	−82	−168	−270	−227	..
Total services, net	**205**	**56**	**7**	**−58**	**58**	**260**
Net factor income[3]	**−1 966**	**−1 957**	**−1 958**	**−2 542**	**−3 039**	**−2 850**
Of which:						
Credits[3]	807	748	782	936	1 272	..
Debits						
Profit repatriation, etc.	1 321	1 320	1 307	1 908	2 337	..
Government debt						
interest	795	761	804	894	973	..
Other debt interest[4]	657	624	629	676	1 001	..
Current transfers, net	**974**	**957**	**879**	**1 011**	**1 109**	**1 319**
Of which:						
EEC[5]	902	891	844	929	1 006	..
Balance on current account	**−650**	**−509**	**239**	**437**	**372**	**540**
Memorandum items:						
Per cent of GNP:						
Trade balance	0.9	2.6	7.2	10.7	10.7	8.0
Invisibles balance	−5.0	−5.6	−5.9	−8.4	−9.0	−5.6
Current account						
balance	−4.1	−3.0	1.3	2.3	1.8	2.4

1. National accounts definitions. Figures for 1990 are projections by the Secretariat.
2. Including passenger fare receipts.
3. Includes remuneration of employees.
4. Including semi-state bodies and banks' interest flows.
5. Excludes certain receipts arising from Ireland's participation in the European Monetary System.
Sources: CSO, *Balance of International Payments*, and *National Income and Expenditure*, OECD Secretariat.

Short-term prospects and risks

The short-term outlook

Recent indicators suggest a prospective weakening in demand and output growth *(Table 6)*. New car sales, having increased by 9 per cent in the first half of 1990, weakened from mid-year, and expectations within the car retail trade are for little net growth in 1991[5]. In the construction sector, housing starts have fallen somewhat, following the rise in interest rates, and the expectation is that housing investment is unlikely to show much growth in 1991[6]. Agricultural construction and commercial development plans are showing similar weakness. Industrial building is likely to be the main source of investment strength, with the EC Structural Fund acting as a stimulus. Due to favourable developments regarding relative unit labour costs and the cost of capital, Irish industry is relatively competitive, and can expect to increase its share of the United Kingdom market, while lower nominal interest rates make for a more favourable investment climate, even though stock prices have fallen by more than they have in the United Kingdom *(Diagram 5)*. One sign of continuing business strength is that the company failure rate has been declining. In general, therefore, there is reason to expect slower growth rather than a recession.

The following technical assumptions underlie the projections given in Table 7:

- A constant effective exchange rate;
- An OECD oil import price of $17 per barrel, compared with an average of just under $26 in the second half of 1990, remaining constant in real terms thereafter;
- An expansion of Ireland's export market for manufactures of 3 per cent in 1991, rising to 6 per cent in 1992;
- Non-agricultural wage rates per head rising by about 5 per cent on average.

A new three-year programme has recently been ratified (a *Programme for Economic and Social Progress,* PESP), which embraces a continuing pay agreement up to 1993[7]. The programme also reaffirms the commitment to maintain interest rates "at the lowest level consistent with international developments and the stable exchange rate policy". This commitment implies that Irish interest rates will be heavily influenced by those in Germany, which are

Table 6. **Recent economic indicators**

Percentage changes from a year earlier

	1987	1988	1989	1990	1990			
					Q1	Q2	Q3	Q4
Manufacturing output	10.4	12.3	11.7	4.7	6.0	4.1	5.8	3.0
Employment								
Manufacturing[1]	−1.1	0.2	2.3	..	3.3	3.7	2.0	..
Building and construction[2]	−14.4	−7.0	9.6	8.3	9.7	9.7	7.5	6.4
Retail sales, volume								
Total	−1.5	2.1	4.7	2.7	3.9	2.2	4.0	1.0
New private car registrations	−7.5	13.9	26.7	6.1	8.4	9.2	4.0	−5.2
Dwellings completed[3]	−10.4	−7.6	21.8	7.2	20.9	12.4	5.0	6.2
Exports, volume	14.2	7.0	11.3	7.9	13.9	7.7	3.2	7.1
Imports, volume	6.2	4.7	12.9	7.1	9.7	10.4	7.8	0.8
Trade surplus (Ir£ million)[4]	1 568	2 090	2 309	1 861	713	496	237	466
Total unemployment rate[5]	18.8	18.4	17.9	17.2	17.6	16.8	17.2	17.3
Average weekly earnings[6]	5.1	4.7	4.0	..	3.1	4.0	3.8	..
Consumer prices	3.2	2.1	4.0	3.4	4.2	3.5	2.9	2.7
Exchequer revenue (Ir£ billion)	7.2	7.7	7.8	8.3	1.9	2.0	2.1	2.3

1. CSO quarterly estimates of employment in industrial establishments with three or more persons engaged.
2. Building employment index for firms in private sector with five or more persons engaged.
3. Number of dwellings completed (excluding local authority dwellings).
4. Quarterly figures are the total of seasonally-adjusted monthly data.
5. Live register total as a per cent of labour force at Mid-April of the same year. Quarterly figures are monthly averages.
6. All industrial workers in manufacturing.
Source: CSO, *Economic Series.*

projected to remain high. Fiscal policy is based on implementation of the 1991 Budget, which aims at an Exchequer borrowing requirement of about 2 per cent of GNP. As is pointed out in the next chapter, this would be consistent with the medium-term objective of reducing the debt/GNP ratio to 100 per cent by 1993.

With employment growth set to slow and net emigration to decline, the unemployment rate is not expected to fall further and could begin to rise again. Inflation is likely to remain low due to the lower oil price and the

Table 7. **Short-term projections**

	1989	1990	1991	1992
	Ir£ million (Current prices)	Per cent changes		
A. Demand and output (volume)				
Private consumption	13 523	3.1	2.5	2.8
Government consumption	3 683	0.0	0.0	0.0
Gross fixed investment	4 320	9.5	4.5	3.9
Final domestic demand	21 526	3.9	2.5	2.6
(Stockbuilding)[1]	90	2.3	0.3	0.1
Total domestic demand	21 616	6.0	2.8	2.6
Exports	15 991	4.9	5.3	6.4
Imports	13 688	7.8	6.0	6.4
(Net factor income paid abroad)[1]	3 039	0.4	−0.6	−0.8
Foreign balance[1,2]	−736	−1.3	−0.8	−0.4
GNP at constant price	20 879	5.1	2.2	2.5
B. Inflation				
GNP deflator		3.6	3.1	3.0
Private consumption deflator		3.2	2.8	2.7
Import deflator		−2.5	2.4	2.2
C. Labour market (thousands)				
Total employment	1 120[3]	2.8	0.7	0.5
Unemployment (rate)	183[3]	14.0	14.3	14.4
D. Balance of payments (US$ million)				
Exports, BOP basis	20 349	24 008	27 055	29 331
Imports, BOP basis	16 311	20 193	23 343	25 352
Trade balance	4 038	3 815	3 712	3 979
Current balance	527	872	575	700
(Per cent of GNP)	(1.8)	(2.4)	(1.4)	(1.6)
	Per cent of GNP			
E. General government				
Net lending	−3.0	−2.3	−2.1	−2.2

1. Contribution to GNP growth.
2. Includes factor income flows.
3. Labour force survey, mid-April, 1990.
Source: OECD Secretariat.

combination of a firm exchange rate policy and a softer labour market. Given the less optimistic outlook for construction, volume growth in fixed investment is likely to slow, but should be sufficient to ensure a continuing rise in the investment/GNP ratio. Under these conditions, real disposable incomes should continue to grow moderately, supporting an increase in real personal consumption of 2½ to 3 per cent. As a result, real final domestic demand should decelerate from 4 per cent growth in 1990 to a rate of about 2½ per cent. GNP growth is likely to be somewhat slower, at between 2 and 2½ per cent, given the slower growth of Irish export markets and the effects of higher interest rates on overseas debt service. Agricultural trade may continue to be affected by disruption in the Gulf and uncertainties over the Common Agricultural Policy, leading to the continued build-up of intervention stocks. EC stocks of beef at the end of 1990 are estimated at 664 000 tonnes, compared with 250 000 in 1989. Purchases in Ireland in 1990 were 233 000 tonnes. Any significant reduction in stocks would require an unrealistically large rise in beef exports to the third world. For budget reasons, therefore, EC support for beef is likely to be curtailed. However, export performance as a whole will be assisted by Ireland's improved international competitiveness. On the assumption that external trading conditions are normalised, 1992 should see GNP growth picking up. Despite a sustained trade surplus, profit repatriations and the rising costs of servicing debt mean the current external surplus is likely to shrink from nearly 2½ per cent of GNP in 1990 to 1½ per cent in 1992.

Risks and uncertainties

The good performance of the Irish economy over the past four years has been the result of a combination of favourable influences which have been mutually reinforcing. These have been: *i)* the confidence engendered by the commitment to narrow-band membership of the EMS; *ii)* the rapid improvement in the budgetary situation; *iii)* the improvement in external competitiveness fostered by the wage restraint agreed under the *Programme for National Recovery*; and *iv)* a favourable world environment of rapid market growth and, in the initial stages of the expansion, declining interest rates. Although the overall environment remains favourable, economic circumstances are in some respects less propitious than they were:

- Interest rate trends in Germany have entailed upward pressure on Irish rates; real interest rates are projected to remain relatively high, and to be susceptible to expectations about the German budget deficit;

- The *PESP* accord has greatly reduced the risk of inflation accelerating and is likely to consolidate recent gains in competitiveness, but public service wage costs are increasing, and with them the relative price of public services;
- Despite Ireland's solid competitive position, the slowdown in OECD area growth is likely to be reflected in a significantly slower growth of exports;
- Public spending pressures, slowing economic growth and higher interest rates are making further reductions in the EBR more difficult;

The possibility that interest rates would need to rise further, as a result of tensions within the EMS, constitutes a threat to the expansion, because Ireland remains highly indebted. Progress on fiscal consolidation could be severely tested if interest rates were to rise above levels assumed in the projection, or if the slowdown in growth were to be more marked. Investor confidence might then be adversely affected. However, more favourable interest rate and market growth trends also cannot be ruled out, so that the risks to the projections seem relatively evenly balanced. The policy background is discussed more fully below.

II. Macroeconomic policy setting

Medium-term financial strategy

Recent years have been characterised by a greater consistency between monetary and fiscal policy, based on the pursuit of two proximate objectives, exchange rate stability and a reduction in the government debt/GNP ratio. Despite an increasingly restrictive fiscal stance, the first half of the 1980s witnessed a rapid increase in government indebtedness, which threatened to become explosive. Tight monetary policy bore the main burden of inflation control, with the credibility of policy gradually being undermined by monetisation pressures[8]. Real interest rates remained very high, exacerbating the debt problem. This unbalanced policy mix proved unsustainable, a fact recognised in the 1987 Budget and Programme for Economic Recovery. A target was adopted to reduce the Exchequer borrowing requirement (EBR) by between 6 and 8 percentage points of GNP in three years. This has been achieved ahead of schedule. Confidence has improved as policies have displayed greater continuity and consistency. Apart from the faster growth noted in the previous chapter, the main benefit has been a marked decline in interest rate differentials *vis-à-vis* Germany.

Greater macroeconomic policy coherence has been easier to achieve because of two factors. The first was the replacement of decentralised wage bargaining by national standard annual pay increases under the Programme of National Recovery. This has helped to increase aggregate real wage flexibility and reduce unemployment, although a comprehensive solution to the unemployment problem also requires removing structural impediments, especially those originating from the tax and benefit systems, an issue to be discussed in the following chapters. The second factor has been the favourable international environment, which has helped to prevent conflicts between short-term objectives arising as a result of the firm exchange rate policy (such as situations involving an unsustainable deterioration in the external balance).

The external economic environment seems now to have deteriorated some-what, due to the slowdown in world growth and the rise in German interest rates. Maintaining a consistent medium-term financial strategy still remains essential to safeguard sustainable medium-term growth, but it provides a formidable challenge.

Monetary developments and the exchange rate

The exchange rate

Monetary policy is implemented within the framework of the narrow band of the Exchange Rate mechanism (ERM) of the European monetary system, which leaves little room for using monetary instruments to pursue other operating targets. Failure to align interest rates to movements in other ERM countries' rates would lead to capital movements and to pressures on either the reserves or the exchange rate. Conflicts can arise where short-term interest rate adjustments run counter to domestic liquidity requirements or the need to maintain the competitiveness of the internationally trading sectors. In the past, whenever the U.S. dollar and sterling were stable *vis-à-vis* the Deutschemark the Irish currency tended to be broadly stable in trade-weighted terms, but movements in these currencies (particularly sterling, which still accounted for around 40 per cent of the trade-weighted index) could cause serious problems for competitiveness. One such episode occurred in 1986 and early 1987, when the pound sterling was depreciating. This caused a loss of competitiveness in Ireland, and raised questions about the EMS parity, which were reflected in higher domestic interest rates needed to stem an outflow of capital. In the first 1986 EMS realignment Ireland kept parity with the ECU, but in August 1986 it devalued. Maintaining a fixed exchange rate policy may thus at times have short-run economic costs. However, sterling's entry into the ERM in October 1990 will moderate fluctuations in the trade-weighted exchange rate index substantially.

In recent years, better inflation performance (especially compared to the United Kingdom), an improving current account and a declining budget deficit have all acted to lend credibility to the fixed exchange rate strategy. Since the beginning of 1989, the Irish pound has generally traded at close to the central rate with the Deutschemark[9]. Movements against the pound sterling and the dollar have thus tended to shadow those of the Deutschemark.

Diagram 11. **EXCHANGE RATE DEVELOPMENTS**

A. Nominal exchange rates
Units per irish pound

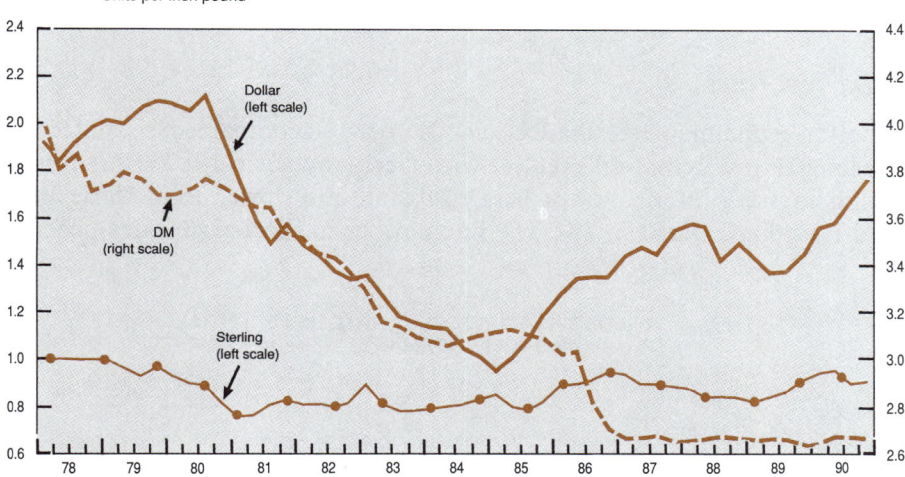

B. Effective exchange rate
1985 = 100

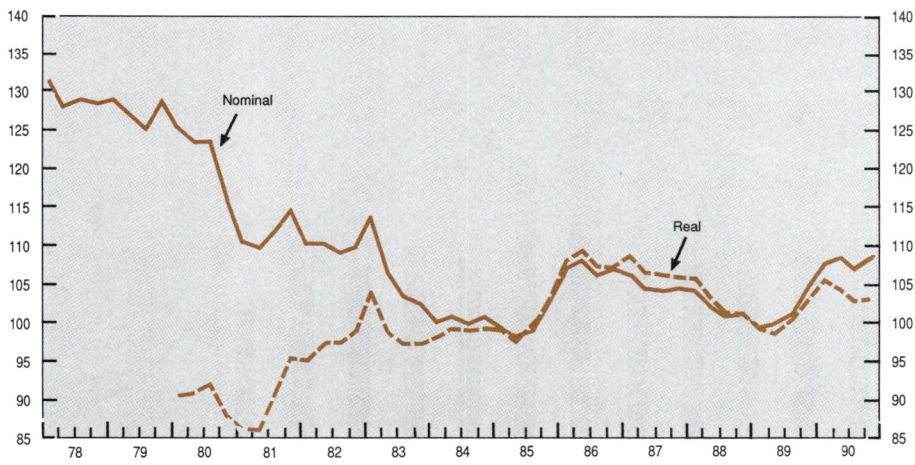

Source: OECD.

35

From the middle of 1989, the dollar began to depreciate against the Deutschemark, as did sterling to a lesser extent. On a yearly average basis, the Irish pound appreciated by nearly 7 per cent in trade-weighted terms in 1990, experiencing an 18 per cent increase against the dollar and 7 per cent against sterling *(Diagram 11)*.

Interest rates

Better economic performance has also been accompanied by a steep fall in the long-term interest differential with Germany since 1987 *(Diagram 12)*, resulting in Irish interest rates being substantially lower than those in the United Kingdom *(Diagram 13)*. The fluctuations in short-term rates needed to

Diagram 12. **LONG-TERM INTEREST RATE DIFFERENTIAL VIS-À-VIS GERMANY**

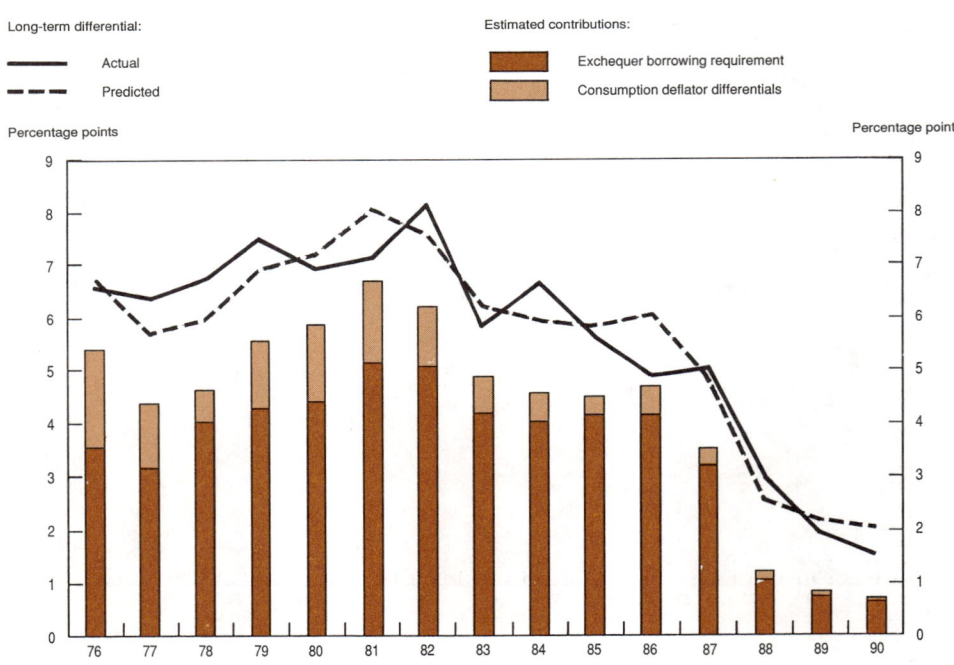

Note: See Technical Annex note for a discussion of the underlying estimation equation.
Source: OECD.

Diagram 13. **INTEREST RATES**

A. Short- and long-term interest rates

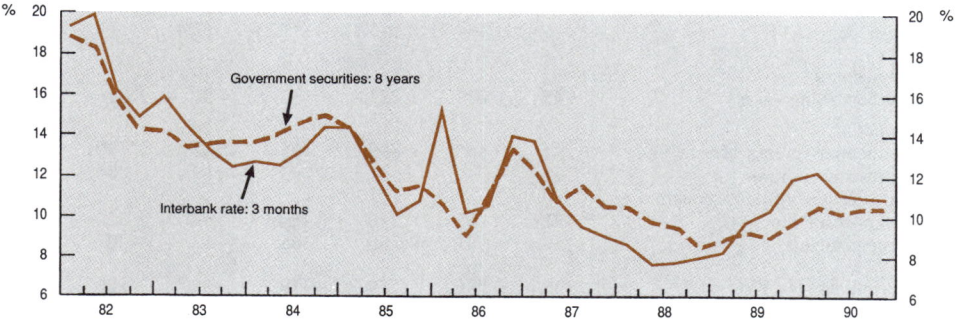

Government securities: 8 years

Interbank rate: 3 months

B. International comparison of short-term interest rates
3 months interbank rate

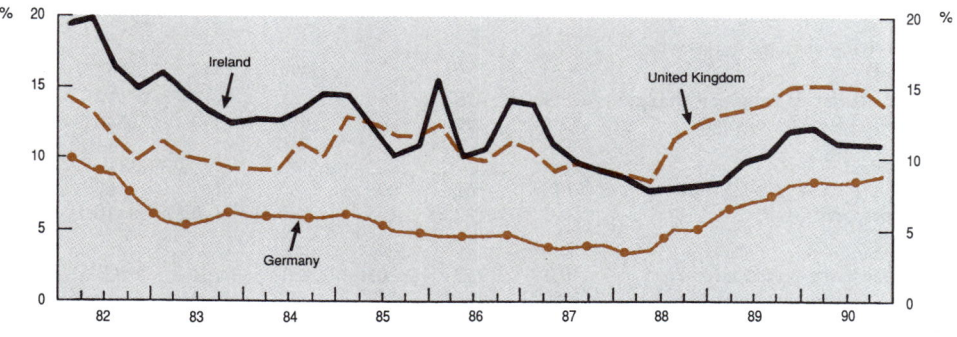

Ireland

United Kingdom

Germany

C. Real interest rates[1]

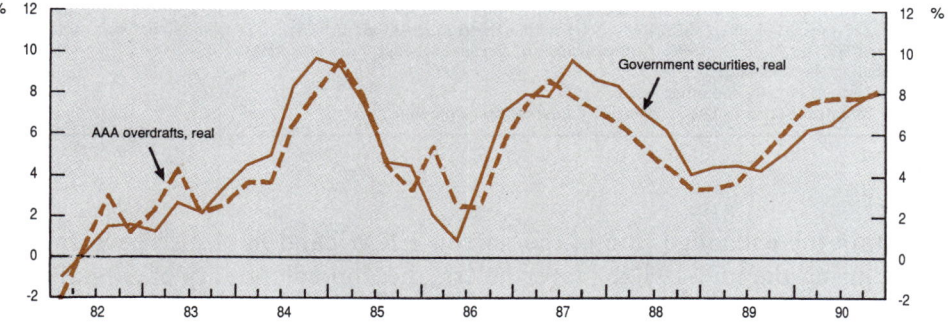

AAA overdrafts, real

Government securities, real

1. Nominal interest rates have been adjusted using the GNP deflator.
Source: Central Bank of Ireland, *Quarterly Bulletin.*

37

Table 8. **Capital account of the balance of payments**

Ir£ million

	1984	1985	1986	1987	1988	1989	1990S1
Current account (= A)	−945	−650	−509	239	437	371	409
(As per cent GNP)	(−6.4)	(−4.2)	(−3.1)	(1.3)	(2.4)	(1.8)	
Capital account							
State borrowing (= X)	945	1 048	1 229	1 188	407	1 046	181
Of which:							
Exchequer foreign borrowing	594	855	899	405	−282	−50	−14
Semi-state inflows	91	19	31	−43	−116	83	53
Sales of government securities to non-residents	121	83	240	460	867	1 320	312
Other official[1]	139	91	60	366	−62	−307	170
Bank inflows[2] (= Y)	368	286	554	−79	365	−186	1 283
Private capital[3] (= Z)	−228	−127	−438	−680	−710	−1 953	−875
Of which:							
Private direct investment	110	150	−30	−	−	−	−
Underlying changes in reserves (= B)	−33	196	−72	606	352	−640	585
Plus: Reserves valuation changes[4]	119	−25	6	11	−13	−	−9
Equals: Reserve changes	86	171	−66	617	339	−640	576
Net residual							
= − [A + (X + Y + Z) − B]	−172	−361	−908	−63	−147	82	413
(As per cent GNP)	(−1.2)	(−2.3)	(−5.5)	(−0.4)	(−0.8)	(0.4)	−
Memorandum:							
Reserves: end-period level	2 101	2 272	2 205	2 821	3 161	2 521	3 097
Swaps, end-period level	50	105	557	40	0	0	−
Reserves, net of swaps	**2 051**	**2 167**	**1 628**	**2 781**	**3 161**	**2 521**	−

1. Net external borrowing by the Agricultural Intervention Agency and change in external accounts at the Central Bank.
2. Includes a valuation effect estimated at (Ir£ million), −63 in 1984, 161 in 1985, 72 in 1986, 90 in 1987, −95 in 1988, 46 in 1989 and 23 in Q1 1990. Also included are foreign exchange swap operations.
3. Excluding the semi-states.
4. Revaluations of gold and other assets.
Sources: Central Statistics Office: *Balance of International Payments.*

maintain the exchange rate in the narrow ERM band have also been smaller than during the mid-1980s. Nevertheless, the unpredictability of capital flows and their changing response to interest rate differentials during a period of decontrol of foreign capital movements have continued to cause problems, and on average the interest rate differential has failed to decline further in the last two years. During 1989, unexpectedly high profit repatriations by foreign firms in Ireland, together with capital outflows related to the relaxation of exchange controls and rising interest rates abroad led to a substantial fall in reserves *(Table 8)*[10]. This necessitated a rise in the Bank's Short-term facility rate (STF), which was increased by 1 percentage point on four occasions, bringing it up to 12 per cent by year end[11]. Increasing domestic demand pressure was also a factor putting upward pressure on interest rates earlier in the year, with house prices rising strongly and private sector credit expanding rapidly. The rise in long rates shadowed a general price decline in international bond markets. However, external reserve losses were the dominant factor in the second half of the year, with the result that for 1989 as a whole the margin of Irish over German interest rates widened considerably.

The main concern in 1990 was to rebuild the official external reserves. Consequently, the higher interest-rate differential was initially maintained. Money market interest rates remained firm in the first quarter, with the three-month differential *vis-à-vis* Germany rising to over 4 percentage points. In the event, net capital inflows from abroad were larger than expected, so that the STF rate was cut by 1 percentage point in June. Following a marked improvement in the level of the official reserves, a further cut of $\frac{1}{2}$ per cent was made in October. Three-month differentials declined, with the premium over German rates falling to about $2\frac{1}{2}$ percentage points in the second half of 1990. The gilt market followed a broadly similar pattern, with a tendency for the yield curve to become less inverted (i.e. for the excess of short over long-rates to narrow). These developments closely followed the pattern of international rates, the integration of world capital markets being such that bond yields have tended recently to vary more in response to world rates than to domestic factors.

Money and credit

Under the present exchange rate regime, money and credit aggregates cannot be treated as independent targets, but they are used as indicators of financial conditions. In 1989, the sharp drop in official reserves and the overfunding of the borrowing requirement both contributed to rather sluggish growth of the money stock as measured by M3: a rise of 5 per cent following a rise of 6.3 per cent in 1988. Since the mid-1980s the financing of the borrowing requirement has been altered fundamentally. The share of monetary financing fell from over 70 per cent in 1984 to 18 per cent in 1988 *(Table 9)*. A net reduction in commercial banks' holdings of government bonds and of direct Exchequer borrowing from abroad were chiefly responsible; increased demand for Irish bonds by foreign investors has facilitated the refinancing of direct external borrowing through sales of domestic-currency-denominated government bonds to non-residents. However, in line with the policy of increasing official reserves, noted above, 1989 and the first half of 1990 saw an increase in monetary financing, back to the absolute levels of 1986 and 1987. In both 1989 and the first half of 1990 the non-bank public were net sellers of government securities, which were taken up mainly by non-residents.

The slowdown in the growth of the money supply in recent years seems also to have derived from portfolio shifts, particularly from a secular increase

Table 9. **Financing of the public sector**

Ir£ million

	1980-84	1985	1986	1987	1988	1989	1990
Exchequer borrowing	**1 693**	**2 015**	**2 145**	**1 786**	**619**[1]	**479**	**462**
(As per cent of GNP)	(14.4)	(12.9)	(12.9)	(10.0)	(3.4)	(2.3)	(2.0)
Monetary financing	**1 193**	**964**	**975**	**873**	**110**	**874**	**201**
(As per cent of GNP)	(10.2)	(6.2)	(5.9)	(4.9)	(0.6)	(4.2)	(0.9)
Direct external government borrowing	888	806	812˙	592	−443	−29	−44
Sales of government bonds to non-residents	(27)	83	241	460	867	1 320	64
Sales of government bonds to commercial banks	260	240	13	84	−130	−214	82
Non-monetary financing	**500**	**1 051**	**1 170**	**913**	**509**	**−395**	**261**
(As per cent of GNP)	(4.2)	(6.7)	(7.1)	(5.1)	(2.7)	(−1.9)	(1.1)
Sales of government bonds to non-bank domestic public	396	680	916	727	170	−556	175
Small savings	103	371	254	186	339	161	86
Other public borrowing	483	429	361	270	132	133	219
Public sector borrowing requirement	**2 172**	**2 444**	**2 506**	**2 056**	**751**[1]	**667**	**681**[2]
(As per cent of GNP)	(18.5)	(15.6)	(15.1)	(11.5)	(4.1)	(3.2)	(3.0)

1. Inclusive of Ir£500 million once-off receipts under the tax incentive scheme (amnesty).
2. Full year projection.
Sources: Central Bank *Quarterly Bulletin*, (various issues); Budget Statement; Department of Finance, *Economic Review and Outlook*; Department of Finance, OECD estimates.

in the share of saving going into long-term institutions *(Table 10)*. Banks, as well as building societies, have suffered a loss of competitiveness in attracting saving deposits, partly because of the tax preferences favouring other financial institutions (see Part IV below). The personal sector is becoming less of a net creditor to the banks in relative terms, and ultimately this entails a greater proportion of bank credit being funded from wholesale market sources or from

Table 10.   **Money supply formation**

Ir£ million

	1981	1986	1987	1988	1989	1990
Domestic credit expansion (DCE)	**2 445**	**1 813**	**1 146**	**1 425**	**2 443**	**1 632**
Of which:						
Monetary financing of the budget deficit[1]	1 442	1 171	703	122	815	273
Bank lending to the non-government sector[2]	1 003	642	443	1 302	1 628	1 359
Total net foreign borrowing[3] (TNFB)	1 210	1 739	155	505	1 711	244
Of which:						
Sales of government securities to non-residents	−30	240	460	867	1 320	64
Direct official foreign borrowing	1 285	812	592	−443	−29	−44
External borrowing by banks[4]	82	620	−281	421	−220	595
Increase (−)/Decrease(+) in official reserves	−127	67	−616	−340	640	−371
Increase in money supply (M3)	1 033	−88	963	622	524	1 690
(Per cent change)	(17.4)	(−1.0)	(10.9)	(6.3)	(5.0)	(15.4)
Memorandum items:						
Domestic credit expansion as per cent of previous period's level of M3	**41.2**	**20.3**	**13.0**	**14.5**	**23.4**	**14.9**
Total net foreign borrowing as per cent of GNP	11.1	10.5	0.9	2.7	8.2	1.1

1.   Includes change in the book value of licensed bank's holding of government securities and hence differs from monetary financing shown in Table 9.
2.   Includes semi-state bodies.
3.   Direct exchequer foreign borrowing *plus* sales of securities to non-residents *minus* change in official external reserves *plus* external borrowing by banks.
4.   Change in net external position of licensed banks, Central Bank Annual Report. Adjusted for banks' participation in foreign currency borrowing by the Irish government and for valuation changes resulting from exchange rate movements.
Note: Using the notation in parentheses, the increase in money supply is defined as: M3 = DCE *minus* TNFB *minus*NDL where NDL are net non-deposit liabilities of the banking system.
Sources: Department of Finance, *Economic Review and Outlook*; Central Bank, *Statistical Supplement*; OECD estimates.

abroad, tending to put pressure on banks' profit margins. Banks are progressively introducing long-term credit instruments to compensate for these developments, but unless existing tax distortions are reduced or eliminated, the current bias against bank credit growth is likely to continue. In 1990 there was a fear that banks would have a problem supplying adequate credit because of slow resource growth. In fact, the expansion of M3 somewhat exceeded growth in private sector credit, weakness in the gilt and equity markets apparently being associated with a greater desire for liquidity by institutions. The banks' liquidity position is set to improve in 1991, as the Budget makes provision for a further considerable reduction in the tax advantages of life assurance-based savings products and a significant easing in bank liquidity requirements has been announced in the 1991 Central Bank Monetary Policy Statement.

Budgetary policy

The 1989 and 1990 Budgets

Between 1986 and 1990, expenditure restraint was the main contributor to fiscal consolidation, as the ratio of the EBR to GNP fell by about 11 percentage points *(Table 11)*. Current expenditure restraint accounted for the major part of the fall, although capital expenditure cuts were also substantial. The ratio of receipts to GNP fell by about 2½ per cent over the same period, as relieving the burden of taxation gained priority[12]. Following the sharp fall in the underlying Exchequer Borrowing Requirement (EBR) in per cent of GNP in 1988, further progress was made in 1989, the EBR falling to 2.3 per cent of GNP (the lowest level for four decades) and the general government financial deficit to 3 per cent. Unexpectedly high revenues and lower debt service expenditure were also partly responsible for this outcome[13]. OECD estimates show that whereas the deficit reduction in 1988 and 1989 was mainly due to a substantial discretionary tightening of policies, the budget deficit correction in 1989 was also greatly assisted by rapid economic growth and a substantial reduction in interest payments *(Table 12)*.

The 1990 Budget projected a further small fall in the EBR to 2.1 per cent of GNP, with the Public Sector Borrowing Requirement (which includes borrowing by state-owned enterprises) expected to rise to 3.5 per cent of GNP

Table 11. Factors behind the fall in the Exchequer Borrowing Requirement

Per cent of GNP, change from 1986 to 1990

	Percentage points
Current budget	
Expenditure	−11.0
Revenue	
Tax revenue	+1.3
Non-tax revenue	+2.1
Total	+3.4
Current deficit	−7.6
Capital budget	
Expenditure	
Public capital programme	−2.5
Of which:	
Sectoral investment	−0.0
Productive infrastructure	−0.2
Social infrastructure	−2.3
Other (non-programme)	−0.5
Total	−2.9
Revenue	−0.2
Exchequer borrowing for capital purposes	−3.1
Total Exchequer borrowing requirement	−10.8

Source: Department of Finance.

compared with 3.2 per cent in 1989 *(Table 13)*. In the event, the outturn for the EBR was 2 per cent and that for the PSBR 3 per cent of GNP, thanks largely to the cyclical buoyancy of the economy. Exchequer returns for the first half of the financial year showed continuing revenue buoyancy (particularly for income taxes), offsetting higher-than-expected capital spending. The non-interest ("primary") budget balance is estimated to have been in surplus by an amount equal to 7¼ per cent of GNP, with debt interest payments amounting to 9¼ per cent and the EBR to 2 per cent of GNP.

The 1991 Budget

On the basis of 5½ per cent nominal GNP growth, the 1991 Budget projects an EBR amounting to Ir£460 million – the same as in 1990 although slightly lower as a ratio of GNP *(Table 13)*. A substantial carry-over of costs

Table 12. **Indicators of fiscal stance**
Per cent of GNP

	1988[1]	1989	1990[2]	1991[2]
General government financial balance				
Financial balance	−7.8	−3.0	−2.3	−2.1
Primary balance	nil	4.3	4.7	4.7
Changes				
Actual	1.5	4.7	0.7	0.2
Cyclically-adjusted	2.2	3.1	−0.4	0.2
Cyclically-adjusted primary balance	2.0	2.8	−0.6	0.0
Memorandum item:				
OECD general government balance	−1.6	−1.1	−1.6	−1.5

1. Excluding the effects of the tax amnesty (an estimated 2.7 per cent of GNP).
2. Based on 1991 Budget.
Note: The general government financial balance, as defined in the National Accounts, is measured in accruals terms. It is commonly used for purposes of international comparison. The EBR (Exchequer Borrowing Requirement) is on a cash basis and measures the deficit for both current and capital purposes in the Irish budget.
Source: OECD calculations.

(mainly transfers) from the 1990 Budget, together with higher interest rates and spending commitments given with respect to public sector pay and the new Programme for Economic and Social Progress *(PESP),* are expected to push up general government spending by about ½ per cent of GNP. The effect of this on the EBR is expected to be more than offset by buoyant tax receipts, especially from the corporate sector. Overall, the Budget has attempted to combine progress towards tax reform and social spending goals with a continuing, steady reduction in the medium-term debt/GNP ratio target. In terms of the public sector borrowing requirement the Budget is, however, slightly expansionary: the PSBR is set to rise from 3 per cent of GNP to 3½ per cent, as prospects for internally-generated sources of finance worsen.

Medium-term consolidation

The primary deficit is depicted in *Diagram 14,* panel A, together with the primary deficit needed to stabilise the debt/GNP ratio[14]. Despite the rapid growth of nominal GNP in the early 1980s – largely due to inflation – the

Table 13. **Budgetary developments**[1]

Ir£ million (per cent of actual GNP)

	1988 Outturn[2]	1989 Outturn	1990 Budget	1990 Outturn	1991 Budget
Current budget					
Expenditure	8 007	8 019	8 387	8 421	9 019
	(42.3)	(38.4)	(38.5)	(37.3)	(37.8)
Of which:					
Interest payments	1 962	1 956	2 108	2 108	2 194
Other current spending	6 045	6 063	6 279	6 313	6 825
Revenue	7 690	7 756	8 130	8 269	8 774
	(40.6)	(37.1)	(37.3)	(36.6)	(36.8)
Deficit	317	263	257	152	245
	(1.7)	(1.3)	(1.2)	(0.7)	(1.0)
Capital budget					
Expenditure	1 362	1 433	1 695	1 684	1 868
Resources	1 060	1 217	1 503	1 374	1 653
Deficit	302	216	192	310	215
Total exchequer borrowing	**619**	**479**	**449**	**462**	**460**
(EBR)	**(3.3)**	**(2.3)**	**(2.1)**	**(2.0)**	**(1.9)**
Total expenditure	9 369	9 452	10 082	10 105	10 887
	(49.5)	(45.3)	(46.2)	(44.7)	(45.6)

1. GNP figures used here are from CSO in 1988-89, and Government estimates in 1990 and 1991 Budget.
2. Figures excluding the estimated once-off effect of the tax amnesty and related factors are 38.0 per cent of GNP for revenue, 4.3 per cent for current deficit and 5.9 per cent for EBR.
Sources: Department of Finance; OECD Secretariat. Further details are shown in Tables F, G and H in the Statistical Annex.

debt ratio expanded rapidly during that period as real interest rates on foreign debt increased[15]. The foreign debt component rose particularly rapidly *(Table 14)*. Since 1983, the the domestic debt component has been the fastest growing, as the "inflation tax" has been eliminated[16], and as the improvement in the primary balance initially failed to keep pace with the increase in debt service. Only since 1987 has the primary surplus risen above the level needed to stabilise the debt/GNP ratio, causing it to decline. In the 1987 *Programme for National Recovery* an EBR of 5 to 7 per cent of GNP was considered to be consistent with the target of stabilising the debt/GNP ratio, given the underlying interest and growth rate assumptions. In the event, the EBR has actually fallen to 2 per cent of GNP, and consequently the debt/GNP ratio has

Diagram 14. **SUSTAINABILITY OF PUBLIC DEBT**

A. Primary balance

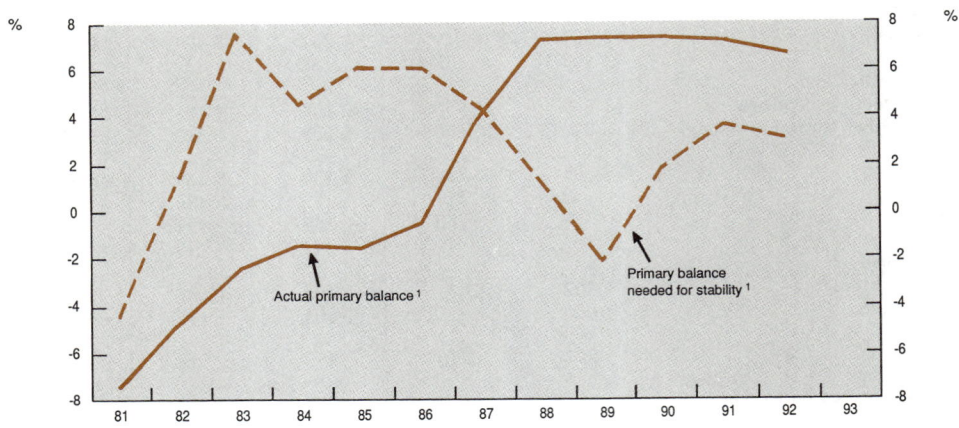

B. Debt and debt interest

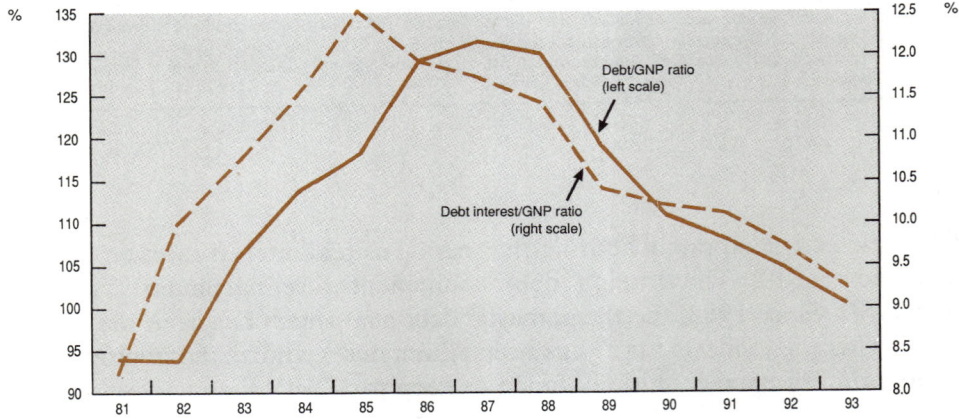

1. Two period moving average of t and t+1.
Sources: Department of Finance and OECD calculations.

46

Table 14. Foreign and domestic debt and debt service
Per cent of GNP

	A. Exchequer debt (net)			
	Foreign debt	Domestic debt	Total debt	Foreign debt as a per cent of total debt
1982	42.1	51.6	93.7	45.0
1983	50.7	55.1	105.9	47.9
1984	53.5	60.2	113.7	47.0
1985	51.7	66.2	117.9	43.9
1986	55.1	74.1	129.2	42.6
1987	53.6	77.4	131.0	40.9
1988	50.1	79.8	129.9	38.6
1989	43.7	75.2	118.9	36.7
1990	39.2	71.9	111.1	35.3
	B. Cost of servicing national debt			
	Foreign interest	Domestic interest	Total debt service[1]	Per cent of government current expenditure
1982	4.1	5.0	10.0	21.2
1983	4.2	5.5	10.7	21.8
1984	4.7	5.8	11.5	24.4
1985	5.0	6.6	12.5	25.8
1986	4.3	6.6	11.9	24.5
1987	4.0	6.7	11.7	25.4
1988	3.7	6.7	11.4	26.7
1989	3.5	5.9	10.1	26.7
1990[2]	3.2	6.1	10.2	27.3

1. Including Sinking Funds and expenses of issue as well as foreign and domestic interest.
2. Provisional outturn.
Source: Department of Finance.

declined more rapidly than initially targeted. It is, however, still the second highest ratio in the OECD area *(Table 15)*.

The aim is to reduce the debt/GNP ratio to 100 per cent by the end of 1993. This programme involves balancing the current budget, which in 1991 is expected to show a deficit of 1 per cent of GNP, while allowing some increase in borrowing for investment purposes, which was disproportionately reduced in the 1980s *(Table 16)*[17]. The target is to be achieved against a background of a prospective medium-term slowdown in nominal income growth, which is likely to be in the range of 5 to 6 per cent, compared to a rate of 9 per cent per annum experienced in the last two years. At the same time, there seems little prospect of German interest rates falling in the foreseeable

Table 15. **International comparison of public debt ratios**[1]

1989

	General government			Net govern-ment external debt	Memorandum: Net investment income paid abroad
	Deficit	Gross debt			
Ireland*	**3.0**	**118.9**	**Ireland***	**43.7**	**14.6**
Ireland	2.7	103.8	Ireland	38.1	12.7
Belgium	6.3	130.8	Greece	24.8	1.0
Italy	10.2	98.4	Denmark	17.7	4.2
Netherlands	5.2	80.9	Sweden	11.6	2.3
Greece	18.4	79.6	Finland	6.4	2.2
Canada	3.4	69.6	Australia	3.5	4.4
Japan*	-2.7	69.3	Norway	3.7	2.9
Portugal	6.6	66.1	Spain	1.3	0.9
Austria	2.7	57.8	New Zealand	1.0	4.1
Denmark	-0.6	54.9			
United States*	1.7	54.0			
Sweden	-5.1	47.8			
France	1.5	46.9			
Spain	2.6	43.1			
Germany*	0.0	43.1			
Norway	-1.2	42.3			
United Kingdom	-0.1	38.6			
Australia	-1.6	14.9			
Finland	-2.9	15.5			

* Indicates ratio to GNP. Others show ratios to GDP.
1. OECD estimates.
Source: OECD; Department of Finance.

future[18]. Consequently, the gap between the interest-rate and the rate of growth of nominal income seems set to widen. In Table 17 a central assumption is made that the differential will average 1½ to 2 percentage points, which would require an average primary surplus of about 7 per cent of GNP from 1990 to 1993 if the 100 per cent debt ratio target is to be achieved. In this case, the EBR could remain at its current level of about 2 per cent of GNP, but would not be allowed to rise above this level. To achieve this, non-interest spending in real terms would have to be very closely controlled.

Debt management and interest rates

Heavy government indebtedness has the dual effect of making the public finances highly sensitive to movements in interest rates[19] while also contribut-

Table 16. **Current and capital spending**

Per cent of GNP

	A. Total public expenditure and taxation (on budgetary basis)					
	Current spending	Capital spending	Total spending	Current revenue	Capital receipts	Total receipts
1984	47.3	13.0	60.3	40.3	7.7	48.0
1985	48.4	11.2	59.6	40.3	6.6	46.9
1986	48.3	10.4	58.7	40.0	5.9	45.9
1987	46.1	9.0	55.1	39.5	5.6	45.1
1988[1]	42.5	7.2	49.7	40.6	5.6	46.4
1989	38.4	6.9	45.3	37.1	5.8	42.9
1990	37.3	7.5	44.8	36.6	6.1	42.7

	B. Components of the Exchequer Borrowing Requirement		
	EBR	For current purposes	For capital purposes
1984	12.4	7.0	5.3
1985	12.8	8.2	4.6
1986	12.8	8.3	4.5
1987	9.9	6.5	3.4
1988[1]	5.9	4.3	1.6
1988[2]	3.3	1.7	1.6
1989	2.3	1.3	1.0
1990	2.0	0.7	1.4
1991[3]	1.9	1.0	0.9

1. Exclusive of one-off receipts under the Tax Incentive Scheme.
2. Inclusive of one-off receipts under the Tax Incentive Scheme.
3. Budget estimate.
Source: Department of Finance.

ing to such movements, because it makes real interest rates more susceptible to speculative attacks on the currency. Exchange control may then be needed: in Ireland's case, high public debt has been one of the reasons for maintaining exchange controls, and debt reduction will facilitate their removal (see Part III). Debt management to lengthen the average maturity, or to smooth the pattern of debt repayment is also an essential element in reducing vulnerability to interest rate fluctuations. Together with the shift towards non-monetary budget financing noted above, attempts have been made to improve the maturity and currency profile of Ireland's foreign currency debt. At the end of 1988, there was a peak in the maturity profile, which meant that some 50 per cent of total foreign debt would be due for refinancing in the four years 1995 to 1998. That peak has now been reduced to 44 per cent. In addition, there has been a switch towards debt denominated in relatively low interest rate currencies which carry little exchange-rate risk[20]. However, Ireland remains rather vulnerable to the costs and risks of interest rate cycles and will probably continue to have to pay a risk premium on borrowing while the debt/GNP ratio remains substantially above the international average[21].

Financial market attitudes towards the EBR probably depend partly on confidence factors related to the level and direction of change in the national debt, principally because long-term interest rates are forward looking. This suggests that progress towards the 100 per cent debt/GNP ratio may have already been discounted in current interest rates. Any slippage would tend to upset financial market confidence and lead to higher interest rates. Given the calculations set out in Table 17, the most visible indication of such slippage would be a projected increase in the EBR above the 2 per cent of GNP needed

Table 17. **Debt dynamics[1]**

Per cent of GNP

| | Change in debt/GNP ratio | Primary balance | | Effect of real GNP growth on debt/GNP ratio[3] | Effect of real interest rate on debt/GNP ratio[3] | Exchequer Borrowing Requirement |
		Actual	Needed to stabilise debt/GNP ratio[2]			
1981	3.0	−7.5	−4.5	−0.8	−3.7	15.9
1982	6.0	−4.8	1.3	0.9	0.2	15.6
1983	9.5	−2.5	7.5	−0.4	8.0	13.6
1984	6.0	−1.5	4.5	−0.9	5.4	12.4
1985	7.8	−1.6	6.1	0.5	5.7	12.8
1986	6.6	−0.6	6.0	−2.8	8.8	12.8
1987	0.4	4.0	4.4	−4.2	8.6	9.9
1988	−6.0	7.2	1.2	−4.1	5.3	3.3
1989	−9.5	7.3	−2.2	−5.6	3.4	2.3
1990[4]	−5.6	7.3	1.8	−3.7	5.5	2.0
1991[5]	−3.5	7.1	3.6	−2.5	6.1	2.0
1992[5]	−3.6	6.6	3.0	−3.0	6.0	2.0

1. Moving average of the current year and the year ahead.
2. See text for explanation.
3. See decomposition in the text.
4. Preliminary estimate.
5. Projections.
Notes: Column 1 = column 3 − column 2;
         Column 3 = column 4 + column 5.
Source: OECD calculations.

to secure the achievement of the official debt/GNP target. Moreover, it is important to note that a fiscal deterioration, like an improvement, can feed upon itself, insofar as the links between interest rates and the deficit are circular and self-reinforcing. Not only do debt and interest rates interact directly, in a way which affects the cost of capital, they also affect the tax burden. The necessity of running a primary surplus implies a heavy opportunity cost in terms of tax reduction possibilities forgone.

III. Medium-term prospects and policy issues

The National Economic and Social Council (NESC) published a strategy for Economic Development (*A Strategy for the Nineties: Economic Stability and Structural Change*) at the end of 1990. Much of this report, like the present *Survey,* is concerned with the need for fiscal consolidation and tax reform. However, the tax system is by no means the only area where structural change is occurring, or needs to occur. Following a discussion of the medium-term prospects for the economy, this chapter looks at the problems of structural adjustment facing Ireland with respect to:

- *i)* The continuing process of financial market liberalisation;
- *ii)* Industrial policies, aimed at attracting foreign capital, and their consistency with the long-run goal of full employment;
- *iii)* The need to improve competition and work incentives in domestic sectors of the economy.

The medium-term outlook

Medium-term projections depend critically on the policy assumptions behind them and, in the case of a small open economy such as Ireland, where over 60 per cent of GDP is exported, on market growth abroad. On the basis of unchanged interest rates (assumed to stay at their nominal May 1990 level), continued pay moderation and zero real growth of the public sector (assumed compatible with an EBR of 2 per cent of GNP), the NESC considers that a 3¾ per cent average annual growth rate of GDP is achievable, so long as Ireland's export markets continue growing at around 5 to 6 per cent a year. This baseline projection incorporates a 7 per cent annual increase in manufacturing output and output growth in the private service sector at half that rate *(Table 18)*. Given relatively buoyant business-fixed investment and

Table 18. **Medium-term projections**

	NESC projections 1991-1994	Historical average 1979-86	1987-1990
		Per cent change, volume	
Expenditure by type			
Personal consumption	3	½	3¾
Fixed investment	5 ¼	−3	7¾
Exports	7	7	8
Imports	6 ¼	2½	7½
GNP	3	¼	4
Output by sector			
Agriculture	1	2½	3¼
Manufacturing	7	4¼	9½
Building and construction	5	..	..
Market services	3.5	..	..
Public services	0	..	..
GDP	3 ¾	1¾	5
		Per cent change	
Employment by sector			
Agriculture	−1	−3¾	¼
Industry	1 ¼	−2½	2½
Private services	1 ¼	1	2½
Total	¾	−¾	1¼
Productivity, total economy[1]	3	2½	3¾

1. GDP per person employed.
Source: NESC, *A Strategy for the Nineties* and OECD calculations.

longer-run strength in the housing market, construction output is expected to grow at an average rate of 5 per cent a year. Agricultural output is expected to expand only slowly. From a supply perspective, 3¾ per cent average annual GDP growth is expected to derive from an average annual increase of ¾ per cent per annum in total employment (all occurring in the private sector), implying a 3 per cent annual labour productivity gain. GNP and national income are assumed to grow at the slower rate of 3 per cent a year, because of a continuing increase in profit repatriation and foreign debt service commitments, both absolute and relative to GDP. With personal consumption assumed to grow in line with income[22], the household saving ratio is projected to remain constant. Since the EBR is projected to stabilise at 2 per cent of

Table 19. **Inputs and productivity in the business sector**

Average annual changes, per cent

	Output (1)	Employment (2)	Labour productivity[1] (3)	Capital stock (4)	Capital productivity (5)	Total factor productivity (6)
Ireland						
1966-73	4.7	−0.2	5.0	2.7	2.0	4.1
1973-79	4.3	−0.6	3.6	4.1	0.2	2.6
1979-87	2.8	−1.1	3.9	3.8	−0.9	2.4
OECD Europe						
1960-73	5.6	0.6	5.0	6.0	−0.5	3.3
1973-79	2.7	0.1	2.6	3.9	−1.3	1.4
1979-88	1.8	−0.2	2.0	2.4	−0.6	1.3

1. Output per employed person.
Note: Column 3 = column 1 − column 2. Total factor productivity (TFP) is equal to the weighted average of growth in labour and capital productivity, with the weight taken as the sample period averages for capital and labour shares; in the case of Ireland the capital share is 30 per cent.
Source: OECD.

GNP, the increase in saving needed to finance the projected increase in the share of investment in GNP would need to come from abroad, implying a corresponding deterioration in the current account balance.

A comparison of expected average economic performance with that experienced over the 1980s provides a convenient starting point for analysing this scenario *(Table 18, Column 2)*. The assumption of 3 per cent total economy productivity growth coincides with the rate attained in the 1979-88 period, but employment growth is expected to average ³/₄ per cent per annum, in contrast to an average annual fall of ¹/₂ per cent a year in the comparison period. The downward trend in public employment during the late 1980s accounts for part of the difference, but both agricultural and industrial employment are expected to perform better than in the preceding period. Employment in the private service sector is expected to continue to grow at a relatively modest rate, as in the past. Prospects for continued output growth depend mainly on the continuing ability to attract foreign direct investment, which has been the basis for the relatively fast growth of the capital stock, together with a continuation of the strong rate of total factor productivity growth which occurred in the 1980s *(Diagram 15 and Table 19)*. However, they also depend on making better use of the large pool of unemployed in the growth process by reducing factor market distortions and rigidities.

Diagram 15. **SOURCES OF GROWTH**

A. **Business sector output**
Annual per cent change

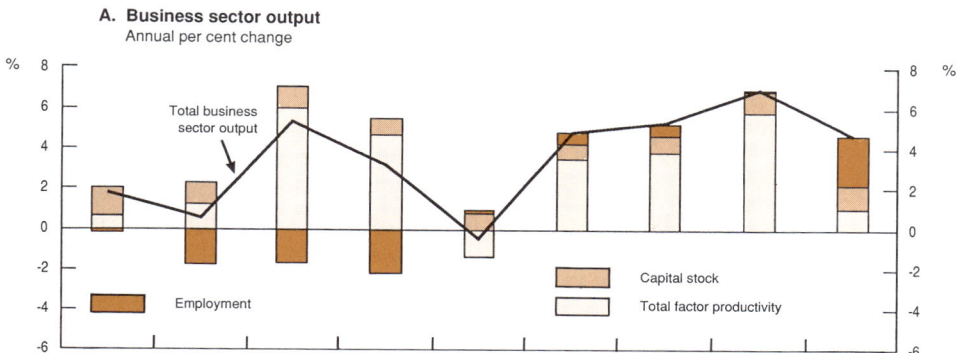

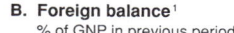

B. **Foreign balance**[1]
% of GNP in previous period

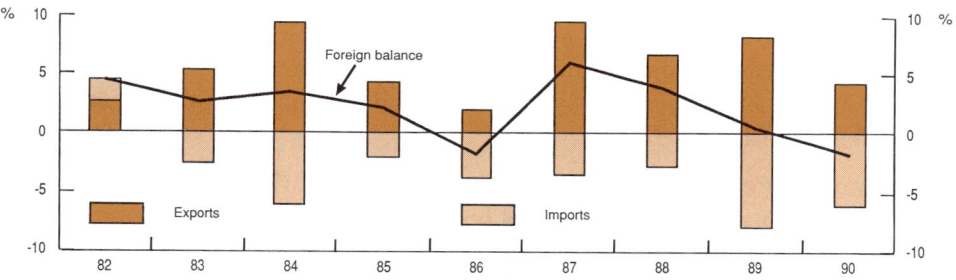

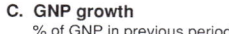

C. **GNP growth**
% of GNP in previous period

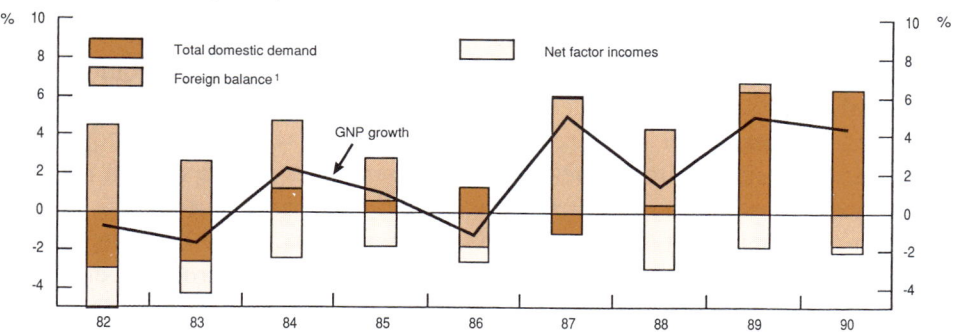

1. Excluding net factor incomes from abroad.
Sources: OECD, *National Accounts;* Secretariat estimates.

Policy issues

Financial market liberalisation and foreign direct investment

The predicted substantial direct foreign investment in the NESC projections relies on the assumption of continued dynamism in the Irish economy, generated by a combination of an unchanged stable macroeconomic policy stance, further European economic and monetary integration and financial market liberalisation. The government is committed to phasing out remaining non-prudential financial market regulations by the end of 1992. Interest rates have essentially been deregulated since 1985; the major remaining exception concerns rates charged to personal borrowers by the major banks, which are felt to have some oligopolistic market power, and it can be argued that the need for this regulation will be reduced as exchange controls are dismantled. Credit ceilings were formally abolished in 1986, leaving few administrative regulations on the banks. Reserve deposits at the central bank are remunerated at close to market rates, and banks are required to invest a fractional counterpart of their eligible liabilities in Irish government securities[23], but in the past banks have consistently held more government stock than required under this provision.

Remaining exchange controls are more intrusive than domestic financial regulations, and their abolition offers both opportunities and challenges. Controls were extended to the Sterling area in 1979 when the EMS arrangements got under way, mainly to prevent the outflow of domestic savings and reduce disruptive international capital flows. Their *raison d'être* has diminished with the improvement in the external and government balances. At a microeconomic level, the main impact of exchange controls is now to distort the pattern of domestic interest rates, and abolition of controls would therefore tend to enhance economic efficiency. Controls over short-term capital movements remain the only restrictions operating *vis-à-vis* EC countries. Limits are placed on direct investment, and purchases of property in non-EC economies. All remaining controls are due to be phased out by the end of 1992. in the context of EC integration. Although exchange controls do not seem to have been a major determinant of the size or direction of direct investment in the past[24], the impact of the abolition on business confidence has potentially important effects on the growth strategy outlined above. On the one hand, it might be argued that controls have helped to prevent excessive fluctuations in interest rates resulting from speculative exchange rate strains within the EMS. Such fluctuations could now occur. However, exchange liberalisation in France and Italy has not been accompanied by substantial downward pressure on their currencies. As long as the abolition of controls is supported by appropriate macroeconomic fundamentals, there is probably little reason to fear additional interest rate volatility, and the abolition of controls could even have beneficial effects on confidence, leading to a further narrowing of interest rate differentials with Germany.

Industrial policy and employment[25]

Weak industrial employment growth has often been noted as the main defect in the industrial development strategy, and there are doubts about sectoral employment creation as a coherent objective of policy. Although the share of employment in manufacturing did not fall by as much in Ireland as it did in the rest of the OECD during the 1980s, the *rate* of employment decline in manufacturing was actually higher than elsewhere *(Table 20)*. Discrimina-

Table 20. **Employment trends**

	1960-73		1974-79		1979-88	
	Ireland	OECD	Ireland	OECD	Ireland	OECD
	Per cent of civilian employment					
Employment in manufacturing	19.3	27.0	21.2	25.2	19.2[1]	21.1
	Per cent growth					
Employment in manufacturing	1.7	1.2	1.2	−0.4	−1.5[1]	−0.6
Employment in services	1.0	2.5	2.5	2.5	1.4[1]	2.3
	Per cent of population from 15 to 64					
Participation rates						
Total	66.5	68.2	62.4	68.5	61.0	70.5
Male	97.6	90.6	89.6	86.6	83.9	83.0
Female	34.7	46.6	34.4	56.8	37.6	58.1
	1980	1985	1986	1987	1988	1989
Memorandum:						
Labour force/population						
Ireland	36.6	36.8	36.9	37.2	37.0	36.7
OECD	45.0	46.0	46.3	46.8	47.1	..

1. From 1979 to 1990.
Source: OECD, *Historical Statistics 1960-88*, Paris 1990, NESC., *A Strategy for the Nineties.*

tion in favour of the export sector, through tax subsidies and other direct government aid, has resulted in strong export growth in recent years (see Part I), but there are doubts about the scale of its net economic benefits. The overall return on capital is rather low (*Table 21*), and the links between the capital-intensive, export-oriented sector and demand and employment in the rest of the domestic economy have remained relatively weak. Capital subsidies have encouraged the substitution of capital for labour, while paying for tax advantages benefiting the privileged sector may have entailed a higher tax rate on domestic sectors (see below).

In the light of these criticisms, and given the need to ensure a reduction in the excessive level of unemployment, the emphasis of industrial policy has

Table 21. **Investment and rates of return in the business sector**

	A. Investment trends Per cent of GDP					
	1960-73		1974-79		1980-88	
	Ireland	OECD	Ireland	OECD	Ireland	OECD
Gross fixed capital formation	**20.7**	**22.0**	**26.1**	**22.2**	**22.3**	**20.7**
of which:						
Residential construction	3.8	5.8	6.0	5.9	5.1	5.1
Non-residential construction	7.4	7.7	6.8	7.6	6.5	7.1
Machinery and equipment	9.5	8.6	13.4	8.7	10.7	8.6
Net national saving	**12.6**	**13.6**	**12.2**	**11.2**	**6.5**	**8.0**
Of which:						
Government net lending	0.7[1]	–0.2	–4.6	–2.4	–7.2	–3.6
Private saving	11.9	13.8	16.7	13.6	13.6	11.6

	B. Rates of return Before tax					
	1975-79	1980-87	1987	1988	1989	1990
Ireland	**4.6**	**5.5**	**7.6**	**7.7**	**9.5**	**9.6**
OECD average						
Smaller economies	11.0	11.0	11.8	12.5	13.0	12.9
OECD Europe	11.6	11.7	12.8	13.3	13.5	13.4
OECD	14.3	14.2	15.5	15.9	16.2	15.9

1. From 1961 to 1973.
Source: OECD, *Historical Statistics 1960-1988*, Paris 1990; *OECD Economic Outlook 48*, Table 56.

now shifted from direct assistance towards, *inter alia,* a greater reliance on repayable forms of aid and grant-assistance linked, to specific performance criteria such as employment, sales and market penetration. It remains to be seen whether this switch to a more selective and conditional industrial policy will succeed in raising total, or even manufacturing, employment. To the extent that the conditions attaching to industrial assistance become more stringent, such assistance is also likely to become less attractive. There is also the consideration that the ability to attract foreign direct investment may depend in part on transfer pricing possibilities which are subject to change by tax legislation elsewhere – or by harmonisation within the EC. There is as yet little sign of the latter, and competition for investment is likely to continue as long as there is an absence of rules to harmonise capital taxes, subsidies and grants among regions of the EC. However, "tax competition" of this sort can prove to be rather cost-ineffective, leading to inefficient tax structures in participating countries, with little – if any – net gain for any of them. Ireland's room for manœuvre on reform of industrial subsidies is influenced by the existence of similar incentives in other regions of the EC, including many which are at a more advanced stage of development.

Public enterprises, privatisation and competition

Domestically, the government retains a large presence in the energy, steel, transport and communications sectors, while also owning some banking and insurance companies[26], hotels, and the national stud. Road, freight and air travel between the United Kingdom and Ireland was deregulated in 1986; the resulting decline in air fares helped to start a major recovery in the tourist industry. However, there is no comprehensive long-term policy of public sector asset privatisation. The government has made it clear that changes of ownership would only occur following consultation with the social partners, and the emphasis has been on improving the commercial performance of public enterprises by imposing stricter financial conditions on investment. The financial position of the public enterprises has improved somewhat since the mid-1980s *(Table 22)*. State subsidies have fallen in real terms, although profits and net worth remain low in relation to gross asset values. The government-guaranteed debt of public enterprises amounted to 25 per cent of GNP at end-1986, but by end-1990 it had fallen to 17 per cent. Over the same period the proportion of the debt of public enterprises which is guaranteed by the government fell from 92 to 76 per cent, in line with government policy of reducing

Table 22. **Performance of state-owned commercial enterprises**[1]

Ir£ million

Year ended	1984-85	1985-86	1986-87	1987-88	1988-89
Profit (loss) account					
Turnover	3 734	3 921	3 834	4 152	4 268
Profit after tax	(24)	79	58	63	156
Extraordinary item	(30)	(28)	(1)	(52)	(60)
Net profit	**(54)**	**51**	**58**	**11**	**96**
Balance sheet					
Fixed assets	3 503	3 721	3 852	4 034	4 131
Investments	2 398	3 037	3 482	3 803	4 508
Net current assets	335	348	278	405	329
Liabilities	5 335	6 048	6 485	6 969	7 553
Net worth	**900**	**1 058**	**1 127**	**1 273**	**1 415**
Performance indicators					
Employment	81	78	75	75	73
State equity investment	81	36	29	11	12
State subsidies[2]	120	116	117	119	112
Dividends/distributions paid	81	95	56	16	17
Corporation tax charge	(3)	(3)	(22)	(33)	(18)

1. The bodies whose accounts are aggregated in this table are as follows:

Energy-related companies	INPC, ESB, BGE and BNM
Industrial bodies	Irish Steel and Siuicre Eireann
Transport bodies	Aer Lingus/Aer Linte, B&I, CIE and Aer Rianta
Banking and insurance	ICC, ACC and Irish Life
Communications bodies	BTE, An Post and RTE
Other companies	Irish National Stud, Great Southern Hotels, Arramara Teo, Racing Board and Bord na gCon.

2. State subsidies almost wholly relate to public transport subsidy.
Source: Department of Finance. The data are based on the latest published accounts for the periods in question.

such guarantees and any potential threat they could pose to the government's goal of further fiscal consolidation.

Labour market rigidities

The institutional characteristics of the labour market were described in the *1987/1988 OECD Economic Survey of Ireland*[27]. A noteworthy feature of the Irish economy has been a markedly weaker employment creation in the service sector than in the rest of the OECD area *(Table 20)*. The NESC projections assume that this relatively slow rate of growth will continue *(Table 18)*. Although the move towards a centralised wage-bargaining system under the PNR seems to have been responsible for increasing the flexibility of real wages in the aggregate[28], an incomes policy may also freeze inter-skill wage differentials in a way inconsistent with relative skill scarcities, thus leading to inefficient resource allocation and imbalances in segments of the labour market. The major benefit of incomes policies is that they may become a useful communications device in a world of imperfect information, communicating rapidly to the social partners what the wage and employment implications of a given macroeconomic policy stance will be. Given such improved information flows, policy misinterpretation can be avoided and transitory adjustment costs reduced. Incomes policies can thus be a useful supplement to appropriate macro-policies, but they cannot substitute for such policies, nor for policies designed to permit appropriate relative wage structures to materialise.

In the Irish case, there is no evidence of any significant tensions arising from specific skill shortages in the manufacturing sector, although the increase in profits has led to calls for a wage catch-up. The weak link is public service pay. The public service wage agreement associated with the PNR expired for most public servants at the end of 1990, and for the commercial state bodies the expiry dates are mainly in 1991. The current arbitration system (which also applies to some public enterprises) is characterised by a high degree of inflexibility, since it gives heavy weight to past pay relativities and pays only limited attention to the employer's ability to pay and overall labour market conditions. This system is in need of review.

Arguably a substantial source of labour market distortions is the tax and benefit system. Replacement ratios for unemployed persons in receipt of Unemployment Benefit (UB) fell in 1987 and 1988, largely due to reforms in pay-related benefits. But long-term unemployment assistance (UA) has been increased significantly. This reflects the policy adopted in the PNR that special provision should be made for those on the lowest welfare payment rates. Increasing employment growth sufficiently to reduce the rate of unemployment necessitates both continued real wage moderation and fundamental structural reform designed to strengthen competition (domestically and through free trade) while removing the work disincentives built into the tax and benefit systems. Taxation is a key area, and is discussed in the next chapter.

IV. Tax reform: an uncompleted programme

Characteristics of the tax system

Concern about the effects of the tax system led to the setting up of a Commission on Taxation in 1980 "to enquire generally into the present system of taxation". At that time the principal concerns were with the distributional and efficiency effects of the tax burden, rather than the level of the overall burden *per se,* which was somewhat below the OECD average. Between 1982 and 1985 the Commission published a series of reports, against the background of a sharply rising ratio of tax receipts to GDP; its increase from 31 to 39 per cent from the late seventies to the mid eighties was three times the OECD average *(Diagram 16, panel A).* Since 1985 better public expenditure control, faster GDP growth and lower interest rates first allowed the tax/GDP ratio to stabilise (between 1985 and 1987) and eventually, after a temporary increase linked to a tax amnesty in 1988, to fall. Tax reform became one of the central elements in the strategy for economic recovery adopted by the National Economic and Social Council (NESC) in 1986[29]. Since then, significant steps have been taken to reduce the tax burden. Together with faster growth, these have reduced total tax revenue to about 38 per cent of GDP (in 1990), which is quite close to the EC average, and only slightly above the average for the OECD. As a ratio of GNP, however, the ratio is significantly higher, at 42 per cent[30].

Taxes on personal income (excluding social security) were the fastest rising component of receipts up to 1988, when the ratio of personal income tax to GNP was 4 percentage points above the OECD average *(Table 23 and Diagram 17).*The share of social security contributions has also been increasing, although it remains at about half of the OECD average. Taxes on property have fallen as a proportion both of total taxation and GNP, following the abolition of the household rating system in 1978. Dependence on this

Diagram 16. **THE TAX BURDEN**
Revenues as per cent of GDP

A. Total tax revenue
Including Social Security

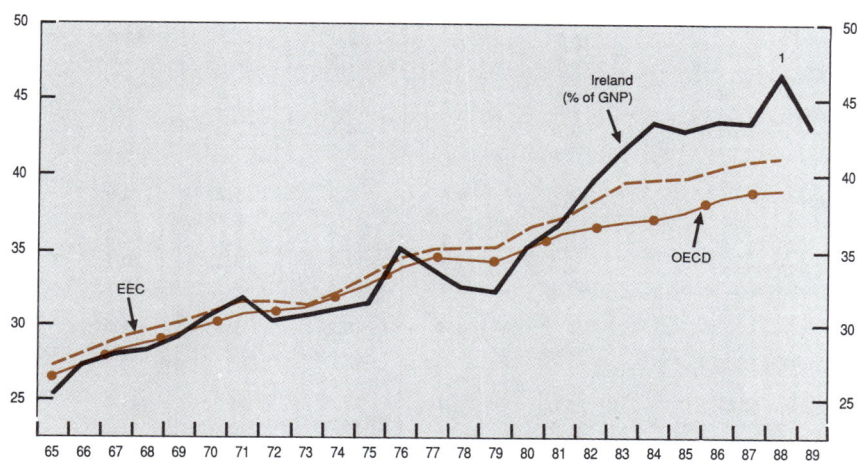

B. Tax revenue
Excluding Social Security

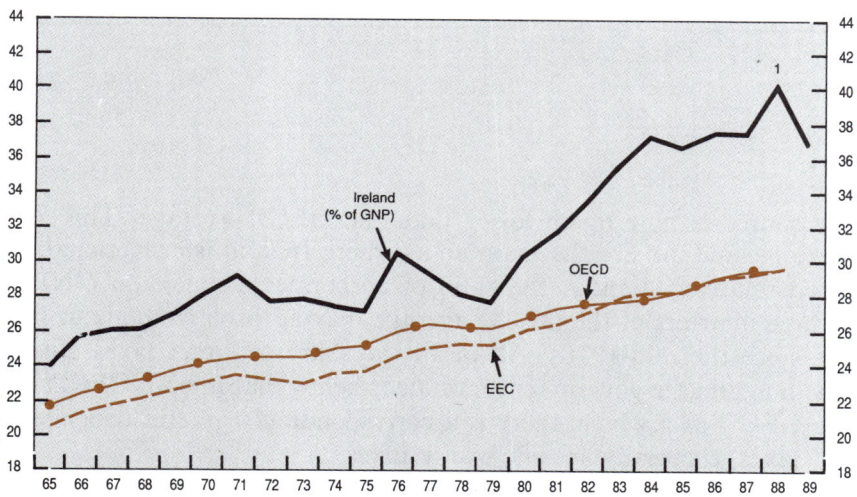

1. Distorted by effects of tax amnesty.
Source: OECD, *Revenue Statistics,* 1990.

Table 23. **The composition of tax revenues**

Per cent of total tax

	1965		1980		1988	
	Ireland	OECD	Ireland	OECD	Ireland	OECD
Income taxes[1]	**25.7**	**35.3**	**36.5**	**39.8**	**38.6**	**38.3**
Personal	16.7	26.3	32.0	32.7	34.8	30.8
Corporate	9.1	9.2	4.5	7.7	3.8	8.0
Social security[2]	**6.5**	**18.2**	**14.3**	**24.2**	**13.9**	**24.2**
Employees	3.2	..	4.7	..	5.1	..
Employers	3.3	..	9.4	..	8.4	..
Property tax	**15.1**	**8.0**	**5.3**	**5.2**	**4.0**	**5.4**
Goods and services[3]	**52.6**	**37.1**	**43.7**	**29.1**	**42.0**	**30.1**
Consumption tax	5.7	11.7	14.8	13.2	20.7	16.4
Specific goods and services	43.4	23.2	28.3	14.2	19.7	12.0
Others	–	**1.4**	**0.2**	**1.7**	**1.5**	**2.0**
Memorandum:						
Total tax						
As per cent of GDP	26.0	26.7	34.0	34.9	41.5	38.4
As a per cent of GNP	26.7	..	35.4	..	47.1	..

1. Personal and corporate income tax do not add up because unallocable taxes are included in the total income taxes in the other countries.
2. Contributions by self-employed are included.
3. Taxes on use of goods and service activities (such as automobile tax) are included.
Source: OECD, *Revenue Statistics, 1965-1989.*

revenue source is now much lower than the OECD average. This and the corporate income tax are the main areas where Ireland is exceptional: profits are taxed relatively lightly, the ratio of corporate tax yield to GNP being about three-quarters of the OECD average, having risen from about half the average since the mid-1970s. All in all the share of direct taxes plus social security in aggregate government revenue is below that in both OECD Europe and the OECD as a whole; there is a correspondingly greater dependence on indirect taxes, especially specific excise taxes.

The relatively heavy dependence on personal income and expenditure taxes has, in turn, been associated with a structure of statutory tax rates which serves to make the overall tax burden heavier than it seems:

Diagram 17. **TAX STRUCTURE**
Composition and share in GDP
1988, per cent of GDP

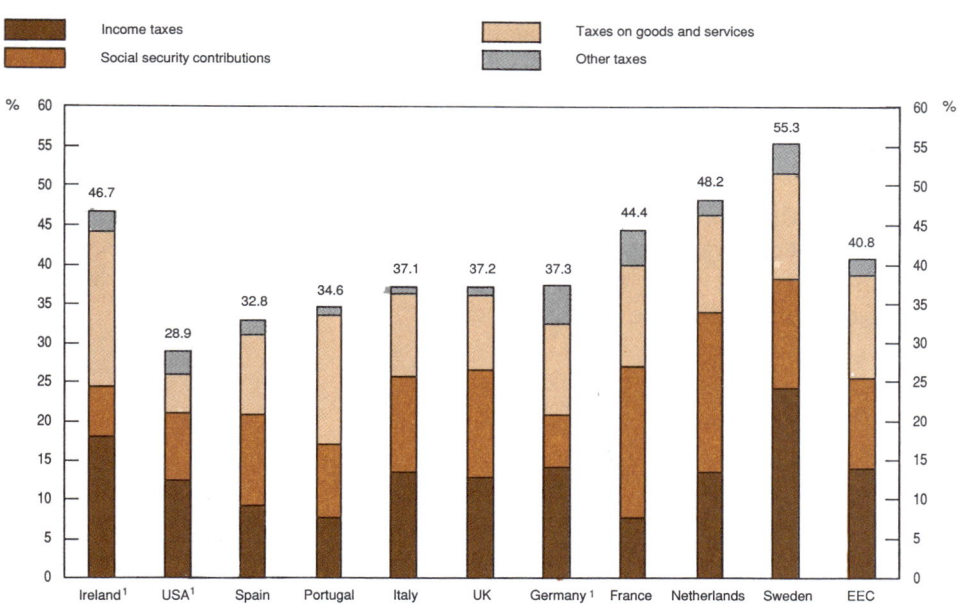

Note: Figures above columns represent total tax shares in GDP.
1. Ratios to GNP.
Source: OECD, *Revenue Statistics of OECD Member Countries.*

i) High expenditures, coupled with the narrowness of the personal
income tax base because of tax exemptions and tax-free income
allowances, has forced tax rates on personal income to levels which
can mean a relatively severe tax wedge at low levels of income,
particularly for single people. The rate of income tax applicable to
single average income earners is significantly higher than in the EC
at large. Special reliefs and exemptions also narrow the bases for the
corporation tax and the VAT, where statutory rates are also higher

65

than in the EC *(Table 24)*. Together with differential treatment of capital gains and corporate income these features can have adverse consequences both for horizontal equity and for the efficient allocation of resources;

ii) The structure of average and marginal tax rates is significantly affected by the interaction of the personal income tax and social security systems, which may exacerbate the problem of high income tax rates.

This Part of the *Survey* begins by describing the extent to which the reforms so far achieved have corrected these defects; it then discusses the economic concerns stemming from biases in the tax system and concludes with an agenda for completing the reform process.

Table 24. **Statutory tax rates**

Per cent

	Statutory rates				Memorandum: EC Average[2]
	Pre 1988	1989	1990	1991	
Personal income tax[1]					
Highest bracket of taxable income	58	56	53	52	53
Intermediate bracket	48	48	48	48	..
Lowest bracket	35	32	30	29	22
Corporate income tax					
Non-manufacturing	50	43	43	43	
Building societies, etc.	35	43	43	43	
Insurance	35	35	35	35	39[3]
Manufacturing	10	10	10	10	
Export sales relief components (to expire in 1990)	0	0	10	10	
Value-added tax					
Standard rate	25	25	23	21	17
Tourism etc.	10	10	10	10/12½	..
Electricity	5	5	10	12½	..
Food etc.	0	0	0	0	..

1. Social security contributions are not included.
2. OECD, *Economies in Transition* 1989. Tax rates are those prevailing in 1988-89. Average for EC less Ireland.
3. Average of standard corporation tax rates; sectoral averages are not available.
Source: Department of Finance; OECD, *Revenue Statistics*, 1965-1989.

Tax reform: motivation and design

The tax reform movement in OECD economies, of which the ongoing Irish reforms are a part, has been based on the pursuit of more economically-neutral (i.e. less discriminatory) tax systems, on the premise that existing systems have imposed excessive efficiency costs for the benefits delivered[31]. Tax systems have developed in an *ad hoc* way, as a result of piecemeal legislation and the impact of inflation, so that the basic principles of efficiency, simplicity, fairness and transparency have been eroded. Given political constraints and competing objectives (with respect to equity for example) a completely neutral tax system would be impossible to design. Nevertheless, the reform movement has aimed at reducing efficiency losses from taxation by moving towards a system which minimises the impact of the tax system on decision-making by economic agents. To achieve this goal three basic rules have been followed:

i) The tax base should be as comprehensive as possible;

ii) A uniform and general consumption tax is more efficient than either selective expenditure taxes or income taxes, the latter being biased against saving;

iii) Where there are several taxes, care needs to be taken to ensure that the interaction between them does not create discontinuities and distortions.

The above discussion has shown that the Irish tax system has been, and remains, in need of reform with respect to all three of the principles cited, and that the redistributive objectives of the tax system could well be achieved while incurring much lower efficiency costs.

The personal income tax

The fact that wages and salaries have traditionally been taxed more heavily than other types of income was one of the primary concerns of the Commission on Taxation, part of whose brief was to suggest ways of achieving an equitable incidence of taxation. In common with many other OECD economies, there was a widespread perception that the tax system was unfair[32]. The Commission's reports set out a wide range of proposals, the general thrust of its recommendations being as follows:

- Income tax was to be charged at a single rate on income arising in the personal and corporate sectors, and applied to a wider and more equitable definition of income, including wages, salaries, profits, realised capital gains, gifts and inheritances;
- The extraordinary range of exemptions and deductions from income was to be replaced by uniform standard personal allowances given in the form of tax credits;
- The tax schedules should be automatically indexed for inflation (including capital gains taxation);
- Tax levied at the company level should be imputed in full to the shareholder receiving dividend payments.

Since 1986 significant progress has been made towards greater equity and administrative efficiency:

- The tax base was broadened and the tax collection system simplified, by the introduction of Deposit Interest Retention Tax (DIRT) in 1986;
- Self-assessment procedures for the self-employed (including farmers) were introduced in 1988, and the incidence of default reduced by enhanced enforcement capability; tax arrears were reduced by a tax amnesty (in 1988) and steps were taken to curb tax evasion and avoidance;
- The value of non-standard tax reliefs has been reduced by cutting mortgage interest and life insurance reliefs and by generally allowing the real value of other reliefs to decline;
- The increased revenues from these measures have helped in reducing tax rates and extending the standard rate band. The number of tax brackets had been reduced to three by 1990 (with marginal rates of 30, 48 and 53 per cent), from six (with rates ranging from 25 to 65 per cent) in 1983 *(Diagram 18)*. The 1991 Budget incorporates further 1 per cent cuts in both the top rate and the standard rate.

Budgetary conditions allowing, the objective is to reduce the standard rate to 25 per cent by 1993, and to move towards a single higher rate of tax.

No formal mechanism has been introduced for adjusting tax brackets and allowances for inflation, with the result that up to the mid-1980s the real value of the higher-rate thresholds was substantially reduced, resulting in "bracket creep" (*Diagram 18*). Since 1986 the standard rate band has been

Diagram 18. **PERSONAL INCOME TAX RATES
AND RATE BANDS**

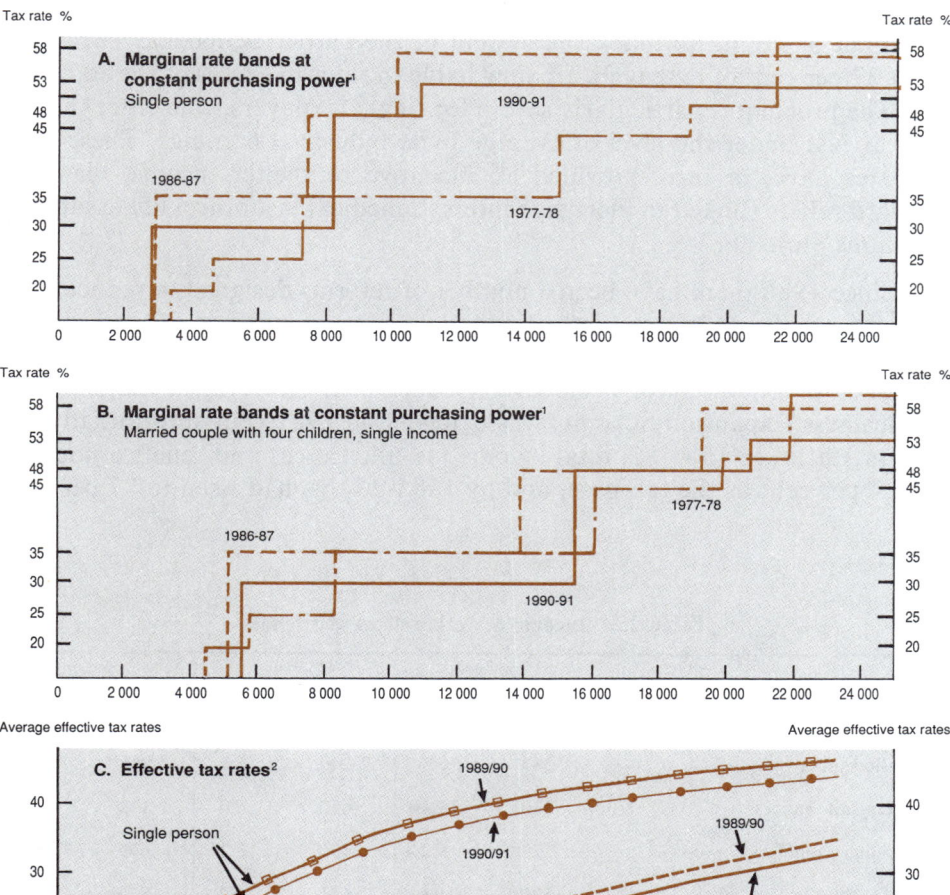

1. 1985/86 prices.
2. Per cent of personal income.
Sources: Department of Finance; NESC, *A Strategy for the Nineties,* and *Budget Documents.*

extended considerably, main personal allowances have been increased and many taxpayers have been taken out of the tax net by raising the exemption threshold beyond which income becomes subject to tax. However, the cumulative effect of failing to index the system in the earlier period has been that about 37 per cent of taxpayers are now liable to rates in excess of the standard rate. The problem is particularly severe for single taxpayers, who enter the top band at just under the level of average male industrial earnings. These high tax rates have, in turn, provided an incentive to shelter income, via non-standard reliefs (linked to mortgage interest, medical insurance, life assurance premiums etc).

Since 1986 there have been a number of reforms designed to reduce non-standard reliefs. Mortgage deductions have been reduced to 80 per cent of interest paid, subject to an (unchanged) ceiling, while deductions for life assurance premiums have been severely curtailed. However, a major relief, the Business Expansion Scheme, was extended in 1987 (but substantially cut back in 1991). In 1981-82, total income tax allowances and reliefs amounted to 62.4 per cent of the tax base, and by 1985-86 this had risen to 77 per cent

Table 25. **Income tax allowances and reliefs**

	1981-82		1985-86		1989-90	
	£ million	Per cent	£ million	Per cent	£ million	Per cent
Basic allowances[1]	1 385	56.3	2 240	55.1	2 986	63.5
Secondary allowances[2]	330	13.4	650	16.0	172	3.7
Discretionary reliefs[3]	227	9.2	495	12.2	699	14.9
Other[4]	520	21.1	681	16.7	845	18.0
Total[5]	2 462	100.0	4 066	100.0	4 702	100.0
Total relief as per cent of tax base	–	62.4	–	76.8	–	68.4

1. Married, single and widowed person's allowances.
2. Allowances in respect of single parent, widowed parent, child, age, housekeeper, dependent relative, blind persons, and employed person taking care of incapacitated individual, nuptial allowance, age exemption limit, general exemption limit.
3. Reliefs in respect of interest, medical insurance, life assurance, permanent health insurance, health expenses, residence-related expenses and artists earnings, exemption in respect of preferential loan and covenanted subscriptions.
4. PAYE (Pay As You Earn) and PRSI (Pay-Related Social Insurance) allowances.
5. Excluding deposit interest exemption.
Source: NESC, *A Strategy for the Nineties.*

70

(Table 25). Subsequent reforms have only reduced this proportion to 68 per cent, so that the conclusion of the recent NESC report was that:

> "Given the modest scale and ambiguity of these changes in the tax base, it is not surprising to find that the income tax base continues to be severely diminished by a wide range of allowances, reliefs and exemptions"[33].

Table 26. **Revenue loss from tax reliefs**

£ million

Tax relief provision	Estimated revenue loss for 1986-87
Income tax	
Relief in respect of medical insurance premiums and health expenses	38.8
Relief for employees' contributions to approved superannuation schemes	44.4
Exemption of the income of approved superannuation funds	62.0
Retirement annuity premiums by self-employed	17.7
Life assurance premiums	32.0
Interest paid in full: purchase, repair or improvement of sole or main residence	152.0
Relief under Schedule E for expenses incurred by employees	13.5
Exemption of interest on savings certificates, national instalment-savings and index-linked savings bonds	13.4
Exemption of income of charities, colleges, hospitals, schools, friendly societies, etc.	15.9
Exemption of Irish government securities where owner not ordinarily resident in Ireland	34.0
Exemption of statutory redundancy payments	10.0
Exemption of payments made as compensation for loss of office	6.25
Exemption from tax of certain social welfare payments:	**237.8**
Of which:	
Children's allowance	59.1
Disability benefit	42.4
Unemployment benefit	24.5
Business expansion scheme	40.0[1]
Income tax and/or corporation tax	
Capital allowances	
Accelerated	170.0
Other	115.0
Export sales relief	377.8
"Shannon" relief	29.0
Stock relief	1.5
Manufacturing relief – reduced corporation tax rate of about 10 per cent	123.5
"Section 84" loans	64.3

1. 1989/90 tax year.

Source: Sixty-sixth Annual Report of the Revenue Commissioners, year ended 1988.

In addition, as for the majority of OECD economies, a large amount of income escapes the tax net altogether, including most fringe benefits, imputed rental income, and all short-term social welfare payments *(Table 26)*.

An extension of the base for social security contributions has been part of the base-broadening programme. A significant proportion of the workforce entitled to social assistance benefits has traditionally made no contribution to the financing of the social welfare system. (In this respect the Irish system has been out of line with other developed countries.) As from 1988, the self-employed (including farmers) became liable for contributions at a rate related to income. The Tax Commission proposed a common tax and social security base, with the social security fund kept separate, but this proposal has so far not been adopted[34]. The combined income tax and contribution system remains complex insofar as there are four different charges: income tax, social insurance, employment and training levy and health insurance contributions. Only the latter two have a common base and contribution rates. Combining the marginal rates of income tax and social insurance contributions makes for a complicated marginal rate structure, with quite high rates being reached at relatively low income levels *(Diagram 19)*[35]. As is pointed out below, the marginal rates are even higher if withdrawal of means-tested benefits is included, although this applies only to a narrow range of income.

Taxation of capital and corporate income

The yields of both capital taxes and corporation tax have been very low by international standards, and have fallen substantially as a percentage of GDP in the last two decades *(Table 23)*. The system of capital taxation has a base that is significantly eroded by exemptions and reliefs. Capital gains on a wide variety of assets are exempt from tax, for example[36]. Contrary to the recommendations of the Commission on Taxation, which was concerned about the erosion of the corporation tax base, new incentives and allowances were introduced up to 1986. Prior to April 1988, business-fixed investment qualified for 100 per cent accelerated capital depreciation allowances for tax purposes, applied in the case of plant, machinery and industrial buildings and representing a significant public subsidy to private investment[37]. Accelerated depreciation is now being phased out by April 1992[38]. Concurrently, the standard corporation tax rate is due to be reduced to 40 per cent from April 1991, which would be broadly in line with the average European rate. Partly because of a switch to self-assessment for corporate income tax, the yield of

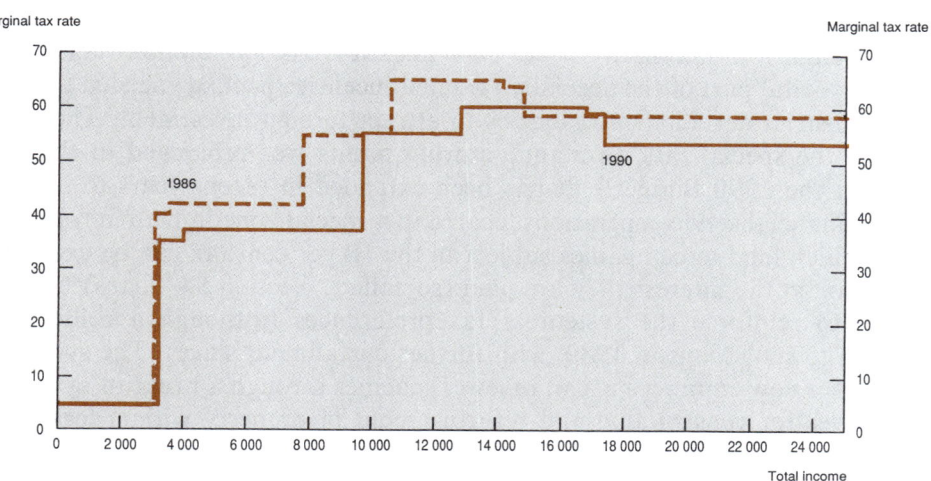

A. Single persons

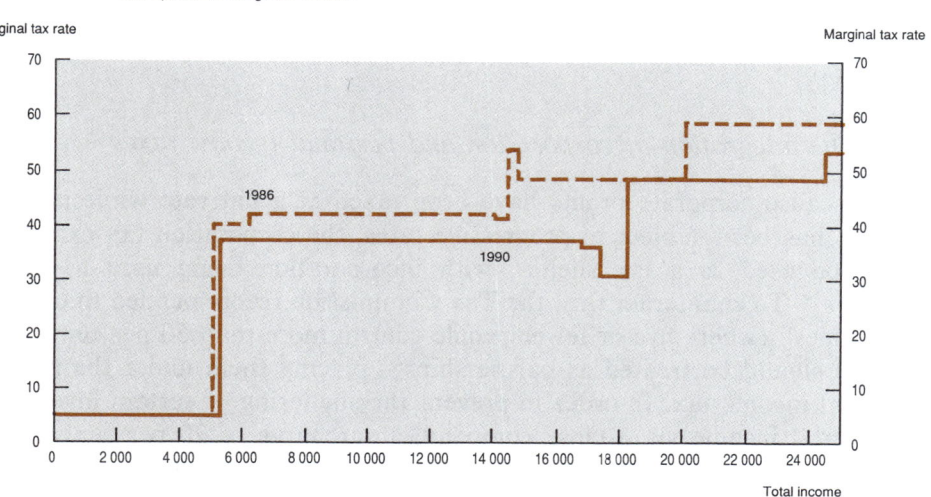

B. Married persons
One spouse working, two children

Source: Department of Finance.

corporation tax has begun to rise. The aim is to increase it further, to provide scope for reductions in statutory income tax rates.

The Tax Commission favoured a single tax rate on profits, equal to the personal income and capital gains tax rate. However, the corporate tax system has been consolidated around a two-rate structure which favours manufacturing through a preferential 10 per cent tax rate. The preferential tax rate is seen as a vital part of the specially targeted incentive package needed to assist the industrial development agencies to attract foreign investment. The duration of the special rate on manufacturing profits was prolonged to the year 2010 in the 1990 Budget[39]. It has been extended in recent years to international financial service operations located in a special zone in Dublin[40]. Institutions which lend to companies subject to the 10 per cent tax can be exempted from tax on the interest they are paid (so-called "Section 84" loans)[41], which serves to reinforce the system of tax preferences (although a ceiling was applied to such loans in 1989, with further curtailment since). The system of incentives now embraces urban renewal schemes through a range of tax-based incentives for construction and refurbishment of property within designated urban renewal areas[42], and the construction of residential property for rent. In conjunction with the entitlement to set losses against income and capital gains in other member companies of the same group[43], such measures have ensured that the cost of capital is both highly subsidised and highly differentiated between alternative investment projects.

The integration of corporation and personal income taxes

Because corporate profits have been taxed at a flat rate while personal income has been subject to progressive rates, the corporation tax can sometimes be used as a tax shelter, with incorporation being used to reduce taxation[44]. To counteract this, the Tax Commission recommended that "close companies" (where five or fewer people control more than 50 per cent of the equity) should be treated as partnerships – placing them under the rules of personal income tax. In order to prevent the sheltering of certain investment and rental income via a close company, a surcharge of 20 per cent applies where such income is not distributed within a certain period. However, a feature of the Irish tax system remains the fact that it permits – both intentionally and unintentionally – leakages out of income tax into lower rates of corporation tax[45]. It is likely that some companies have been incorporated only to obtain the benefits of lower tax rates. Of the estimated Ir£320 million yield from corporation tax in 1989, 60 per cent was paid by narrowly-owned ("close") companies, leaving only Ir£128 million of "true" corporation tax (just above 1 per cent of total revenues)[46].

The Commission also criticised the distortions that arose because the tax system effectively taxed company distributions twice – first as company income and then as personal income. Double taxation may affect corporate financing behaviour and the cost of capital (see below). In Ireland the problem is substantially relieved by a partial imputation system, which allows 50 per cent of the corporation tax to be credited against income tax. The Commission recommended that the imputation rate should be raised to 100 per cent and that a withholding tax be levied on company distributions. The latter proposal was implemented in 1983, but with only half of the corporation tax on distributed profits credited to the investor. This puts Ireland in a group, including France and the United Kingdom, which mitigates but does not eliminate double taxation *(Table 27)*[47]. Moreover, the taxation of profits is complicated by an unusually complex capital gains tax, which operates with three different rates, ranging from 30 to 50 per cent.

Consumption taxes

Following the recommendation of the Commission on Taxation, significant progress has been made in simplifying the VAT system. By 1990, the number of statutory rates had been cut to three (including a zero rate) and the standard rate reduced from 25 to 23 per cent. It has been further reduced to 21 per cent in the 1991 Budget[48]. This is still about 4 percentage points above the EC average *(Table 23)*, while VAT exemptions make for a rather differentiated pattern of effective tax rates on consumption *(Table 28)*. Excise rates are relatively high, although their real value has fallen in recent years in anticipation of EC harmonisation. The indirect tax system is now under review as part of the preparations for the single European market. In its 1989 proposals, the EC commission proposed a standard VAT system with a minimum standard rate (informally set at 15 per cent) and a reduced rate band of 4 to 9 per cent applicable to specified basic goods and services. Minimum rates were also set for excises, with longer-run target rates above these minima proposed as the ultimate objective. The changes required in existing Irish rates to meet EC harmonisation objectives will depend on the overall shape of the final package, as yet unsettled. However, to prevent cross-border revenue losses, Irish tax rates will need to be brought closer to those in the United

75

Table 27. **Integration of corporate and personal income tax in OECD countries**

Degree of double taxation of distributed profits due to the fact that dividends are also subject to income tax in the hands of shareholders

No integration	Partial integration		Full integration	
	Corporate level	Shareholder level	Corporate level	Shareholder level
Classical system	Partial deduction of dividends paid	Partial credit for corporate tax paid	Full dividend and deduction system or zero rate on distributed profits	Full credit for corporate tax paid (imputation system)
	Lower tax rate on distributed profits			
Luxembourg	Germany	Ireland	Greece	Australia
Netherlands	Japan	France	Norway	Germany
Switzerland	Portugal	United Kingdom		Italy
United States	Finland	Denmark		New Zealand
	Iceland	Austria		Turkey
	Spain	Belgium		
	Sweden	Canada		
		Japan		

Source: OECD, Department of Fiscal and Financial Affairs.

76

Table 28. **VAT rates by consumption category**

Per cent of total consumption

Consumption categories	Tax exempt[1]	VAT rate				Total
		0[1]	10	12½	21	
Food	–	17.82	–	3.49	3.57	24.88
Alcohol and tobacco	–	–	–	–	14.94	14.94
Clothing and footwear	–	1.05	–	5.55	–	6.60
Fuel and light	–	–	–	5.95	–	5.95
Housing	6.21	–	0.72	–	0.71	7.64
Household and other goods	–	1.07	2.21	0.06	7.83	11.17
Transport	4.14	–	–	0.67	9.42	14.23
Services	8.46	–	0.19	3.90	2.04	14.59
Total	18.81	19.94	3.12	19.62	38.51	100.00

1. Zero-rated items receive rebates of VAT paid at intermediate stages of production. Exempt categories do not.
Source: Department of Finance.

Kingdom (where the standard rate is now 17½ per cent). Reductions in some excises will be needed to achieve EC harmonisation, although cultural, social and environmental considerations will mean that national differences in tax rates will persist. However, the pace of convergence will also be heavily determined by overall budgetary and economic circumstances and requirements.

Economic effects of reform: some specific issues

The economic effects of tax distortions are impossible to estimate directly, since they depend on individual preferences and the degree of substitutability between factors of production. However, following a discussion of the progressiveness of the Irish tax system, three of the most important aspects of the impact of taxation on efficiency are discussed below:

- *Tax wedges and employment*: taxes can affect the choice between work and leisure, with possible repercussions for employment and unemployment;

77

- *Investment and the cost of capital:* the tax code has heavily subsidised business fixed investment, with the aim of fostering growth. In so doing, some activities have been favoured over others, with unpredictable, but probably adverse, efficiency consequences;
- *Taxation and saving:* the tax system incorporates several selective incentives to save, the effect being to shift savings into tax-favoured financial sectors and investment categories, without necessarily increasing the total volume of saving.

In assessing the economic effects of tax reform, a principle derived from general equilibrium analysis is that economic distortions will be greater the higher is the marginal rate of tax and the wider the dispersion of tax rates. The cost of assisting one sector in preference to another has to be measured not just in terms of tax revenue forgone, but should take account of the less efficient allocation of resources used.

Effects on income distribution

In a tax system which provides possibilities to shelter income, high statutory tax rates do not necessarily lead to effective tax progressivity[49]. A rising marginal rate schedule is usually the source of efforts to avoid tax[50]. In the case of Ireland the potential for this problem would seem to be quite substantial, given the large number of tax payers – some 37 per cent – liable to the higher statutory tax rates. Despite recent reforms, single tax payers (with only standard allowances) enter the top tax bracket at incomes below the average level of male industrial earnings. At the same time there remains the possibility of sheltering income from higher tax rates through discretionary tax reliefs, which can reduce progressivity at higher income levels. The implication would seem to be that a reform which further reduced such reliefs while reducing rates and revising the higher rate thresholds would make the personal income tax system both more efficient and more progressive.

The interaction of the tax and social benefit systems can mean, for some married couples on low incomes, that higher gross pay is not reflected in disposable income. Family Income Supplement (FIS), which adds significantly to net income at low levels of earnings, thereby increasing incentives to take lower-paid work, is withdrawn rapidly as income rises. Over a Ir£2 000 range of gross earnings, the FIS falls from Ir£988 to nil – an effective marginal benefit rate of –50 per cent. At certain income levels there are also discontinuities due to means tests: as earnings rise local authority rents rise for example. These benefit conditions exacerbate the tax rate effects noted above *(Diagram 20)*. The type of low income trap illustrated applies only to a very small proportion of the employed workforce (³/₄ per cent). The existence of such anomalies and their severity are extremely sensitive to the specific procedures and calculations adopted[51]. However, the interaction between tax and benefit systems may, in principle, create severe work disincentives for specific segments of the labour force.

Diagram 20. **THE LOW-INCOME TRAP**[1]

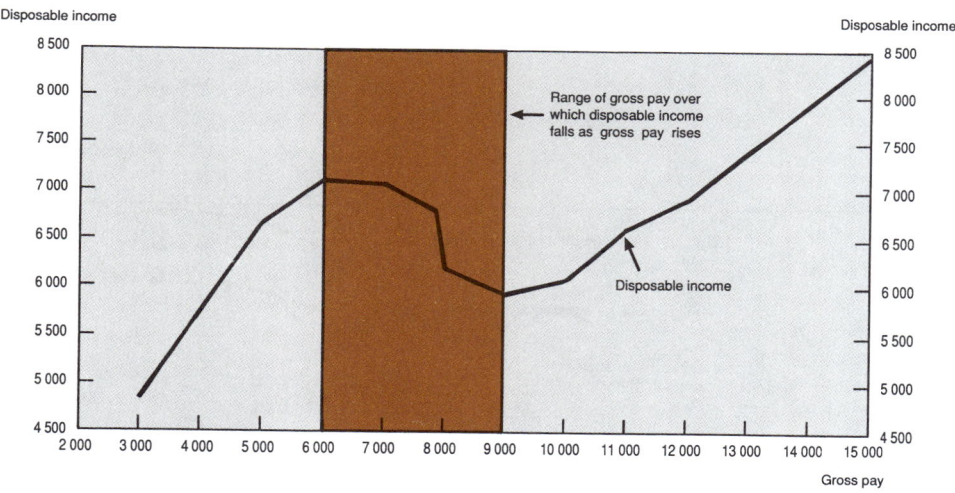

1. Man, wife, four children, 1989/1990, per annum; for explanation see Annex.
Source: Department of Finance.

Tax wedges and the labour market

Taxation affects the labour market by driving a wedge between the cost incurred by firms in hiring workers (the "product wage") and the wages received by employees (the "consumption wage"). Income, payroll and indirect taxes all affect the wedge, so that in respect to work incentives indirect taxes have no advantage over income taxes. In Ireland, the tax wedge was one of the highest in the OECD area in the early 1980s, the overall marginal tax rate on labour use of 70 per cent being the fourth-highest after Sweden, Denmark and the Netherlands[52]. The average tax wedge increased in the first half of the 1980s, as real labour costs to firms rose and real after-tax wages fell *(Diagram 21)*. The gap has begun to narrow somewhat since 1987. But despite recent reforms, the marginal tax on labour income (measured at the average production-worker wage) is still among the highest in the OECD area.

The impact of the tax wedge on employment and unemployment cannot be identified with precision. However, the relatively heavy dependence on taxes on labour income has provided an incentive to substitute capital for

Diagram 21. **THE TAX WEDGE**

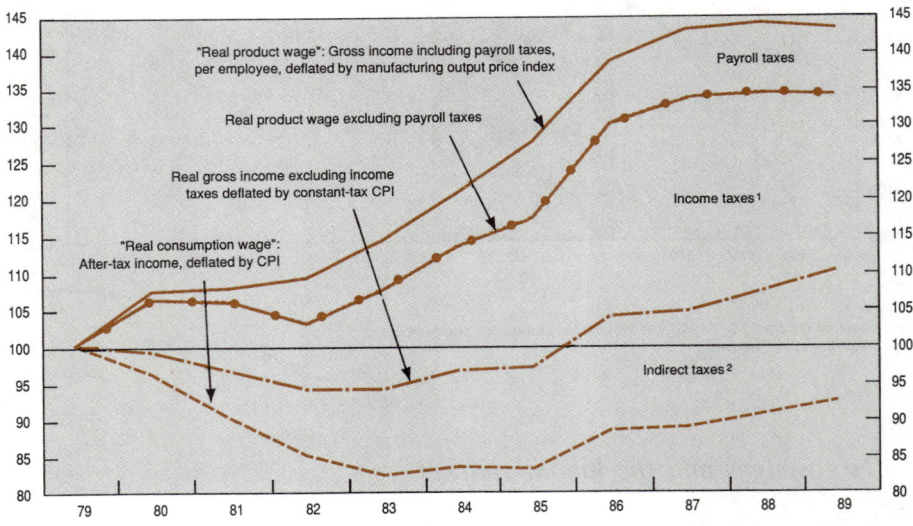

1. Includes net social security contributions.
2. Includes terms of trade effects.
Source: OECD; for details see Technical notes.

labour which has discriminated against domestic service industries and probably impeded employment growth in that sector (see *Table 20*). The tax and social security wedge may also have had an adverse effect on labour force participation rates, emigration and unemployment:

- Participation rates have been in decline for many years, partly reflecting the growing proportion of young people in education and higher state pensions. The downward trend in male participation rates has been stronger than the OECD average, while the increase in married women's participation has been relatively small *(Table 20)*;

- Taxation may also have been a factor in the increase in emigration during the 1980s *(Diagram 2, panel 4)*. The secular shift in emigration, described in the 1988/89 *OECD Economic Survey of Ireland,* has been

Diagram 22. **REPLACEMENT RATIOS**[1]

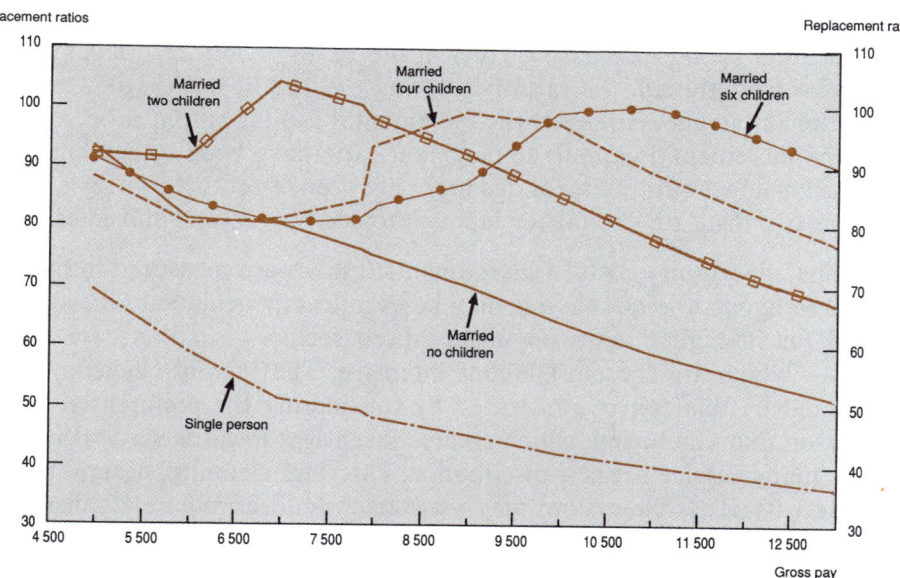

1. Disposable income of persons receiving long-term unemployment assistance as a percentage of net pay. The data refer to the tax/benefit year 1989/1990 and all figures are post-Budget 1989.
Source: Department of Finance.

81

associated with a high propensity to emigrate among highly-qualified workers. This results in an increase in the dependency ratio, which increases the burden on the working population;
- Despite measures to improve the net income of low-paid employees, "income replacement ratios" for the unemployed with families remain rather high *(Diagram 22)*[53].

The increase in long-term unemployment in Ireland during the 1980s was proportionally the largest in the OECD area, and those out of work for a year or more now account for about one-half of all unemployed.

Investment and the cost of capital

Empirical studies of the cost of capital in Ireland show that the influence of the corporate tax system has been very significant, and at least partly responsible for increasing the cost of labour relative to capital in the manufacturing sector[54]. As noted, the Irish company tax system has provided some of the most generous subsidies to business investment in the OECD area[55]. The ratio of machinery and equipment investment to GDP, having been relatively high since the 1960s, increased further in the 1970s *(Table 21)*. In contrast to trends observed abroad, the ratio fell during the 1980s, but is still above the international average. However, the incremental capital-output ratio, and still more, the incremental capital/employment ratio have been rather high. The job-creation effect of investment has probably been offset, in large part, by the incentive to substitute capital for labour provided by capital subsidies.

If the opportunity costs of investment subsidies are measured in terms of tax cuts foregone, the net pay-off may be even less evident. Subsidies have to be paid for in higher taxes on unsubsidised sectors – in this case mainly services – which are the most labour intensive. The type of efficiency losses engendered by this can be illustrated by considering the preferential 10 per cent tax on manufacturing, which creates incentives towards vertical integration. In many service areas – distribution, catering, cleaning, design, promotional activity etc – the system may inadvertently discriminate against "contracting out" by the manufacturing sector[56]. Such discrimination may involve substantial costs where it leads to unexploited economies of scale or specialisation. It is officially estimated that the manufacturing investment subsidy programme has induced Ir£350 million worth of projects, entailing 8 000 construction jobs. Jobs may also have been indirectly created in the service sector. But in general, service-producing industries have been adversely affected to an unknown extent by the structure of incentives.

Impact on saving patterns

i) Differential tax treatment

The Tax Commission concluded that the the personal sector enjoyed significant tax incentives to borrow, while the taxation of saving was often heavy[57]. In particular, income tax relief for interest on loans for non-business purposes was relatively generous, while levying tax on nominal interest earnings made real rates of return to lenders negative in the then highly-inflationary environment[58]. Moreover, the structure of exemptions and other reliefs in respect of saving had built up in a haphazard way and had become extremely complex, with little or no rationale in terms of either equity or efficiency. The Commission concluded that equity and efficiency would be best served if existing distortions in the market for loanable funds, introduced by differential tax treatment, were eliminated. In the particular case of life assurance relief, the Commission saw no evidence that the investment performance of life assurance funds was superior in economic and social terms to that undertaken by other institutions, and suggested withdrawing tax relief. In the case of pension funds, relief for superannuation contributions and exemptions for the earnings of pension funds contrasted favourably with the tax treatment of an individual who saved privately and acted to reduce labour mobility where pension rights were incompletely transferable. The 1990 Pensions Act has addressed this problem by providing for the transfer of accrued pension rights when an employee changes jobs.

The principle that the tax system should not try to affect saving decisions is based on the recognition that an efficient tax system is one where relative rates of return on all forms of saving (allowing for risk) are unaffected by taxation. More practically, it derives from the difficulties of assessing the exact effects of complex and discriminatory tax rules. In Ireland, effective tax rates on some forms of saving, particularly deposits taxed under the DIRT, may be high, while certain types of capital gains are often exempt from tax. The tax system thus encourages the creation of devices which convert interest income into capital gains resulting in tax avoidance. Differential tax treatment has led to the evolution of a privileged saving sector, based on sheltering

Table 29.   **Personal financial assets by institution**

Per cent of total

	1961	1970	1980	1987
Banks	45	38	34	27
Building societies	2	15	31	7
State agencies	21	20	3	9
Life assurance/pension funds	31	27	32	57

Source: D. de Buitleir, *A Four-year Programme of Tax Reform in Ireland*, Allied Irish Banks, October 1989, unpublished paper.

income, especially from the higher rates of tax. Flow of funds data document an increasing share of institutional saving in the personal sector's gross acquisition of financial assets, which began in the mid-1970s and accelerated in the 1980s *(Table 29)*. Parallel to this trend, the proportion of government and corporate securities purchased by life insurance companies and pension funds has increased dramatically[59].

Some aspects of the tax treatment of savings have been changed significantly. Relief for interest payments and life assurance premiums have been restricted, for example. But the tax treatment of instruments and institutions through which people can save is still highly selective and discriminatory *(Table 30)*. The introduction of the Business Expansion Scheme (BES), whereby tax relief is allowed on amounts subscribed for shares in companies in certain sectors of the economy has tended to make the saving incentive system even more interventionist, although the 1991 Budget measures aim to redirect it to its original purpose as a source of equity finance for small companies. The scheme had become a tax-sheltering device involving investment in secure asset-backed ventures with little risk. A recent review of the Irish tax system concluded that there is still a large degree of variation in the tax treatment of saving, and that the system "diverges significantly from the principles of neutrality and equity"[60].

ii)   Corporate finance

In some cases, new saving incentives have been introduced to offset distortions arising elsewhere in the tax system. The BES scheme may be

Table 30. Tax treatment of saving

Asset/saving instrument	Tax treatment
Interest-bearing accounts	
National savings	Exempt.
Bank deposits	Prior to 1986, interest taxed at owner's marginal tax rate; since 1986, interest taxed at source at standard rate under DIRT, with higher-rate tax payers obliged to make up difference between DIRT and relevant higher rate.
Building Society deposits	Prior to 1986, interest taxed at source under composite rate method, with higher-rate tax payer obliged to make up difference between composite and higher rate: since 1986, interest taxed at source at standard rate under DIRT, with higher-rate tax payer obliged to make up difference between DIRT and relevant higher rate.
Marketable assets	
Gilts	Interest taxed at owner's marginal tax rate. Capital gains – exempt.
Shares	Taxation of dividends depends on the rate of corporation tax paid by the distributing company. Capital gains: – Exempt to 1974. – 1974-78 nominal CGT. – 1978 real CGT. Shares purchased under the Business Expansion Scheme qualify for relief against income tax subject to a limit of Ir£25 000.
Indirect holdings	
Pension funds	Contribution relief (up to ceiling). – Fund income exempt (6 per cent tax for 1988). – Pension payments taxable with tax-free lump sum.
Life assurance policies	Relief on one-eighth of premium (up to ceiling). – Investment income subject to income tax. – Proceeds tax free to policy holder.
Real assets	
Private residence	Imputed rent and capital gains exempt. Property taxes (rates) abolished 1977. – Mortgage interest relief (80 per cent, subject to a ceiling).

Source: R. Thom, *The Taxation of Savings*, Foundation for Fiscal Studies, 1988.

viewed in this light, as a means of increasing the supply of risk capital in the face of a tax system which may not favour the further development of an equity market. The combined effect of the corporation tax, income tax and capital gains taxes is to make equity investment by individuals relatively unattractive (especially compared with gilts, which are exempt from capital gains tax). Moreover, since long-term capital gains are taxed at a lower rate

Table 31. **Effective tax rates on gross dividends**[1]

Per cent

Shareholder's marginal tax rate	Proportion of profits retained				
	0.00	0.25	0.50	0.75	1.00
Company paying 43 per cent corporation tax[2]					
0[3]	20.8	26.4	31.9	37.4	43.0
35	48.5	47.1	45.7	44.6	43.0
58	66.3	60.8	54.8	48.9	43.0
Company paying 10 per cent corporation tax[4]					
0[3]	5.0	6.3	7.5	8.8	10.0
35	21.6	18.7	15.8	12.9	10.0
58	32.6	26.6	21.3	15.6	10.0

1. Assumes zero inflation, or capital gains less than the rate of inflation (in which case they are untaxed).
2. Tax credit = 28/72; see Annex.
3. Applies to indirect holdings via "tax exempt" institutions such as pension funds.
4. Tax credit = 1/18; see Annex.
Source: R. Thom, *op. cit.*

than distributed profits, there is an incentive for firms to reduce capital costs by relying on internal sources of finance. Investing out of retained earnings is more tax-efficient for the shareholder than distributing and re-borrowing, since capital gains tax is inflation-adjusted and the effective rate of tax falls as the retention ratio rises *(Table 31)*.

iii) Subsidies to owner-occupied housing

The privileged tax position enjoyed by house-owners also has an effect on saving patterns, since there is an incentive for households to hold a high proportion of wealth in the form of residential property. The only local tax currently in operation is a property tax on commercial buildings, the taxation of residential property having been abandoned in the 1970s. The taxation of imputed rent from owner-occupation was also abolished in 1969. Mortgage interest deductibility remained, while capital gains on owner-occupied housing have always been tax exempt. The tax system has thus been highly favourable to investment in residential property. The Tax Commission advocated that mortgage interest deductibility be phased out, except for first-time buyers. Reform has been rather more cautious, with 80 per cent of interest paid now being deductible, up to a ceiling. Insofar as the imputed rent is untaxed, interest payments are still mostly deductible and there is virtually no residential property tax, the Irish tax system remains one of the most generous towards housing investment *(Table 32)*. The effect has been to stimulate

Table 32. **The tax treatment of income from home ownership in OECD countries**

No tax on imputed rent		Tax on imputed rent		
Full interest deductibility	Interest deductible up to a ceiling	Interest deductible		No deductibility
		No ceiling	Ceiling	
No or negligible tax on residential property				
	Ireland[1]			
	United Kingdom	Denmark	Italy	
Tax on residential property				
United States	Australia	Belgium	Finland	Canada
	Austria	Germany	Greece	
	France	Netherlands	Spain	
		Norway		
		Sweden		

1. Only 80 per cent of interest within ceiling is deductible.
Source: OECD, *The Personal Income Tax Base, a Comparative Survey*, Paris 1990.

demand for housing, raising the proportion of personal wealth held in the form of property. However, favourable tax treatment for housing tends to become rather rapidly "capitalised" into the price of housing and land. In this way it probably achieves little for first-time buyers.

Agenda for further reform

Although significant reforms have been undertaken in the past few years, the tax system is still characterised by rate structures which distort the allocation of resources. As regards the personal income tax system, the main remaining imperfections are:

i) Tax rates are relatively high at low-to-middle income levels. Single taxpayers may be taxed at the highest rate at levels of income below the average male industrial wage;

ii) There are still a significant number of discretionary reliefs, the benefits of which are probably outweighed by the costs in terms of narrowing the tax base and raising statutory tax rates;

iii) Tax neutrality with respect to owner-occupied housing decisions would require the inclusion of imputed rent and real capital gains (less interest and maintenance costs) in the income tax base;

iv) The yield from farm incomes remains unsatisfactory insofar as (the move to self-assessment notwithstanding) only a minority of farmers are liable to tax.

To achieve a standard rate of personal income tax of 25 per cent by 1993, with a single higher rate of tax, which is the government's declared goal, the discretionary allowances and reliefs built into the system need further overhaul. Options for broadening the personal income tax base would include discontinuing deductibility of various saving instruments (e.g. life assurance premium[61]) and bringing short-term social welfare benefits and lump-sum retirement benefits within the tax net[62]. A Fringe Benefit Tax (following the Australian and New Zealand model[63]) would also help to restore that part of the tax base which has been eroded by the provision of fringe benefits.

Disincentives resulting from the interaction of the income tax and social security transactions call for particular consideration, although the distinction between the purposes of the social security funds and general tax revenues needs to be maintained. Long-term social welfare benefits (such as pensions) are subject to income tax, but short-term benefits are not. Correcting the omission would both raise revenues (an estimated Ir£52 million) and improve efficiency, by increasing the incentive to take up employment. Such a step is often opposed on the grounds that it would be regressive. However, calculations made by the ESRI show that 70 per cent of those affected would be in the upper half of the income distribution, and less than 10 per cent of those affected are in the bottom three deciles[64]. The equity argument for non-taxation of short-term welfare benefits is thus difficult to sustain.

Combining the income and social security systems on the basis of a standard rate of 30 per cent and a top rate of 50 per cent would cost a net Ir£700 million (3 per cent of GNP) after the elimination of special tax reliefs, according to ESRI calculations, made on the basis of 1987 figures[65]. The integration of the two systems on this basis would offer considerable advantages over the current system, although this would represent a departure from the regimes which apply in nearly all OECD member states, where separate contributory systems are the norm. Revenue losses from lowering personal tax rates could to some extent be compensated by increasing taxation of corporate profits and broadening the tax base by including property and reducing the scope of measures, such as the Business Expansion Scheme, which act as tax shelters.

The complete omission of residential property from the tax base is difficult to justify in economic terms. Indeed, since the base for a national property tax would be immobile (in contrast both to local property taxes[66] and to the more elastic direct and indirect tax bases) a property tax would be relatively non-distortionary. According to one calculation, a property tax could yield about Ir£430 million, equivalent to 7 percentage points off the standard rate of income tax[67]. Failing the introduction of a residential property tax, or the inclusion of imputed rent for owner-occupied housing in the tax base, the phasing out of mortgage interest relief would be appropriate, both to restore neutrality between owner-occupied and rental property and to permit reducing taxes on labour income. The fact that mortgage interest relief, like life assurance and medical insurance reliefs, is concentrated in the upper end of the income distribution means that there could also be some desirable distributional implications from such a reform[68].

The corporation tax also offers scope for improvement, since the cost-effectiveness of capital subsidies is to be questioned. If they are truly marginal – i.e. given to new entrants who would not otherwise have invested in Ireland – they would be self-financing, in the sense that tax subsidies depend on the profits actually made. It is, however, difficult to devise a system of incentives which does not involve either the government forgoing current revenues from corporation tax or relieving the investor from part of the commercial investment risk. In either case, subsidies have long-run budgetary costs which exacerbate the impact of the high tax wedge on labour. This extra burden may generate distortions and inefficiencies which outweigh the returns from greater foreign direct investment in Ireland. In an open economy investment should normally be carried to the point where returns equal the world interest rate, and if the returns are lower, the country would be better off investing abroad, or – as is the case with Ireland – paying off its debt. Tax subsidies might be justified where there are associated social benefits which do not accrue to the private investor (e.g. regional investments, or selective support to basic research), or where foreign investment results in a longer-run transfer of technology and know-how. However, if employment creation is the aim, a more effective method of creating employment would be to increase the yield of corporation tax and cut income taxes.

While increasing the yield of corporation tax is important to reduce personal tax rates, the company tax system also needs further reforming in other respects, so as to:

- Ensure greater neutrality *vis-à-vis* business organisation;
- Achieve greater neutrality between debt and equity finance and between profit retentions and distributions.

To meet these objectives, the personal income and corporation tax systems should be more fully integrated, by allowing full imputation of the standard rate of tax[69]. One of the arguments against increasing the imputation rate is revenue loss. However, as noted, some companies succeed in sheltering all of their profit tax liabilities apart from that paid on distributions, which is the most difficult tax liability to avoid.

Commitments to harmonise indirect tax rates with those in the EC will cause significant revenue losses. Reducing excises in the context of tax harmonisation may also pose a problem. In addition, it seems unlikely that Ireland can maintain a standard rate of VAT more than a few points above that of the United Kingdom (17½ per cent), given the ease of movement between the two countries, and each percentage point reduction would cost Ir£65 million in a full year. However, there remains the need for further rationalisation in indirect tax rates in the interests of economic efficiency, independent of the level of rates at which this occurs.

V. Conclusions

The strengthening of stabilisation policies in 1987 and 1988, discussed in the *1988/89 OECD Economic Survey of Ireland,* has been followed by a rapid and impressive improvement in macroeconomic performance. The favourable international environment in which these policies have been implemented has helped to contain the costs of adjustment often associated with such programmes. While GNP growth has accelerated, the inflation differential *vis-à-vis* Germany has been all but eliminated, and the interest rate differential has substantially narrowed. The reduction in the public debt/GNP ratio has coincided with a boom in manufacturing output and business investment. While profitability has improved, real personal incomes have also increased. Following a period of declining employment, the pace of private sector job-creation has increased. However, the unemployment rate – though declining somewhat – has remained exceptionally high, both by historical and international standards, representing a major challenge to economic policy.

Greater consistency between the different areas of macroeconomic policy has played an essential part in the recovery:

- The commitment to narrow-band membership of the Exchange Rate Mechanism (ERM) has acted as an effective nominal anchor for anti-inflationary monetary policy;
- Confidence and competitiveness have been enhanced by the general adherence to the non-inflationary pay terms of the *Programme for National Recovery (PNR)*;
- The decline in the Exchequer Borrowing Requirement (EBR) has removed one of the main factors sustaining inflation expectations, while the consequent reduction in the debt service burden has also facilitated the recent easing in tax pressures. These developments have been an essential part of the inflation-reduction process.

As a result, the Irish pound has traded at near to its central parity with the Deutschemark in the last two years, without the need for marked fluctuations in interest rates. The exchange rate commitment implies a risk that monetary conditions will be tighter than required by domestic conditions because of the need to follow interest rate trends abroad. However, this has not been an important factor in the past two years.

Short-term prospects are marked by an external environment that is becoming less favourable, principally because Ireland's major trading partner, the United Kingdom, and the United States, are in recession. Consequently, the combination of macroeconomic adjustment and good economic performance is becoming harder to achieve. GNP growth could be halved to between 2 and 2½ per cent in the next two years. Moreover, the anticipated increased demand for credit to finance eastern and central European – particularly East German – reconstruction has put upward pressure on real interest rates in Europe, with adverse consequences for the budget balance, the current external account and business fixed investment. In such circumstances employment growth can be expected to ease and inflation to decline further. The *PNR* expired at the end of 1990, and a new three-year wage agreement has been ratified *(Programme for Economic and Social Progress (PESP))*, which provides for an average increase of 3½ per cent a year up to 1993, with the possibility of negotiating supplemental increases averaging up to 1 per cent a year at local level. No marked tensions seem to have built up in the private sector under the PNR, and the ability to negotiate locally has added a degree of flexibility to the wage-formation process. Provided such bargaining takes full account of competitiveness and related issues – as envisaged – employment and inflation prospects should be enhanced. The PESP terms also apply to public sector employees. However, pay rises deferred under the PNR will entail increases in public sector wage rates during 1991 and 1992 significantly above those in the private sector.

The combination of slowing external demand growth, higher real interest rates and increasing public sector wage costs mean that Ireland will find it more difficult to sustain the pace of fiscal and economic progress attained over the past few years. The fact that Ireland is in a relatively good position to gain export market shares on account of competitiveness developments should mitigate the slowdown in export demand. At 111 per cent, the public debt/ GNP ratio is still the second-highest in the OECD area, and as a result the overall budget deficit is very sensitive to interest rate movements. The future course of interest rates remains uncertain, and could be favourable. However, an increase in debt service costs because of interest rate pressures in the EMS would constitute a serious threat to the ongoing fiscal consolidation efforts.

Maintaining a financial strategy which creates favourable conditions for sustainable (i.e. non-inflationary) medium-term growth is essential. The government has declared its intention to reduce the public debt/GNP ratio to 100 per cent by 1993. The achievement of this goal – and a continuing decline thereafter – is important to safeguard the gains already made in terms of lower inflation and interest rates, and would help improve the conditions for further growth. It is probable that the new target has already been discounted by financial markets. If so, any slippage would tend to upset confidence, leading to higher interest rates, slower growth and cumulative pressure on the EBR. The maximum permissible EBR consistent with the debt/GNP target depends on parameters which are to some extent uncertain, particularly the differential between interest rates and growth rates. But given the risk of adverse shocks, borrowing should not exceed an average of 2 per cent of GNP over the next three years. In normal circumstances, automatic stabilisers might be allowed to come into play as growth slows down, but since even temporary deficits add to outstanding debt, flexibility in this regard is severely limited. The Budget already incorporates a rise in public spending relative to GNP in 1991, so that any deficit slippage might be interpreted as a failure to control government expenditure. Beyond 1991, it is equally important that implementation of the discretionary elements of the PESP which involve higher public spending be limited to whatever can be undertaken within this fiscal constraint.

The Government's ultimate economic policy objectives are to narrow the substantial gap in living standards between Ireland and the European average, and to bring the unemployment rate down to a more acceptable level. The successful pursuit of these objectives has important implications for microeconomic policies. Better exploitation of the growth and employment opportunities created by coherent macroeconomic policies requires further structural reform, notably in the areas of industrial policies, and in taxation and other policies impacting on the labour market.

Industrial policies relying on tax privileges and direct subsidies have in the past succeeded in attracting high-tech, export-oriented manufacturing enterprises. But these policies, besides having only a limited spillover into domestic sectors of the economy, have involved costs which have contributed to a heavy tax burden on labour. They have also helped to create a distorting tax structure, with differential tax rates for different activities. One effect of such policies has been to retard the development of an efficient domestic service sector. Furthermore, they have distorted relative factor prices in favour of capital in an economy characterised by a large excess supply of labour. The recent scaling down of industrial subsidies and the phasing out of accelerated depreciation allowances, together with the reduction in the standard corporate tax rate, have helped to reduce such distortions. Given the undesirable side effects of these policies and the continuing need for fiscal consolidation, the ongoing process of reform should be continued.

With the Irish unemployment rate the second highest in the OECD area, policies that create distortions in the labour market require special scrutiny. High replacement ratios (social benefits as a ratio of net earnings) provide little incentive for some low-skill unemployed to seek employment. Recent measures to improve net incomes of low income earners have begun to address this problem. However, in the process they have increased effective marginal tax/benefit rates for low income earners. It is important to co-ordinate carefully tax and benefit schedules to minimise the efficiency losses created by any given level of taxes and social benefits. On this account further progress seems both possible and necessary.

Although in recent years Ireland has been visibly successful in attracting foreign investment and developing a competitive export-oriented manufacturing sector, it has been less successful in fostering competition in the domestic economy. Policies towards privatisation of state-owned industries have been relatively cautious, and efforts to improve the commercial performance of public enterprises have had only limited results. Although the financial position of the public enterprises has improved, and state subsidies have fallen in real terms, this sector remains a potential drain on public resources. Furthermore, in some cases wage awards are determined by arbitration, which is insufficiently sensitive to labour market imbalances and productivity developments. An overhaul of management structures, including a more aggressive approach towards privatisation of public enterprises, would contribute to fiscal consolidation, competition and economic efficiency.

While progress has been made in bringing about lower and more uniform tax rates, and in broadening the tax base generally, Irish statutory rates are still high by international standards. Thus, further reform of the tax system could yield additional efficiency gains. Concerning personal income tax, high marginal rates still affect a large proportion of tax payers (becoming operative at fairly modest levels of income), stifling effort and initiative and inducing enterprising and skilled members of the labour force to emigrate. The restriction of special allowances, exemptions and reliefs which narrow the tax base, complicate the tax code and reduce allocative efficiency needs to be continued, if rates are to be reduced further. Among the various options for broadening the tax base in general, the least distorting seems a tax on residential property. The virtual omission of residential property from the tax base is difficult to justify on economic grounds. An additional rationalisation of the indirect tax base is also called for. The standard rate of VAT, although significantly reduced recently, remains high and will need to be brought down as fiscal frontiers are dismantled in the EC. However fiscal harmonisation is likely to result in significant revenue losses. Reform of taxation has to be accompanied by action to extend the tax base generally to prevent slippage with respect to the fiscal consolidation target.

One of the reasons why the burden of income tax and expenditure taxes is currently so heavy is the fact that the yields of both capital taxes and corporation tax are very low, despite significant recent increases. The current structure of these taxes suffers from a number of defects, apart from the bias against labour noted above:

- Incorporation provides some opportunity for tax deferral by the personal sector, particularly via the preferential corporation tax;
- The interaction of corporation, capital gains and income taxes biases corporate financing decisions and creditors' choice of saving instruments. For companies liable at the standard rate (40 per cent), equities are treated less favourably than debt finance or retained earnings.

The company tax system is thus in need of reform, so as to raise more tax revenue from this source, and to ensure greater neutrality *vis-à-vis* capital and labour, between methods of corporate finance, and between decisions about corporate structure. A start has been made with the phasing out of accelerated depreciation provisions, but the prolongation of the 10 per cent manufacturing rate to 2010 has greatly reduced flexibility in that area.

Personal saving decisions are likewise affected by the tax system in a number of ways:

- Institutional (especially life assurance and pension fund) saving is favoured over alternative forms of personal saving;
- Certain tax-based incentives, such as the Business Expansion Scheme (BES), have tended to channel saving into tax-sheltering devices, without adding to the pool of domestic savings;

- Bank and building society deposits are relatively unattractive due in part to the deposit interest retention tax;
- Capital gains tax exemptions encourage the practice of converting interest and profit income into capital gains;
- The privileged tax position enjoyed by the housing sector also has an effect on saving and investment patterns, since there is an incentive for households to hold a high proportion of wealth in the form of residential property.

While recent reforms have reduced the importance of several of these distortions, the taxation of saving still diverges significantly from the principles of neutrality and equity and is in need of overhaul.

With a significant improvement in Irish economic performance having been achieved in the last few years, it is essential that macroeconomic policy continue its commitment to exchange rate stability and public spending restraint. This policy stance needs to be supplemented by a programme of structural reform, if output and employment growth are to continue at satisfactory rates and the gaps between Irish and average OECD unemployment rates and living standards are to be reduced. Structural reform is all the more important because the immediate benefits of the consolidation efforts in the form of lower interest rates, lower inflation and greater business confidence have already been achieved, while the impulse from favourable world trading conditions is diminishing. Structural reform has so far concentrated on financial liberalisation and tax reform. Efforts now need to be made to step up and broaden the process, while consolidating the gains made in reducing the debt burden. Persistence with the considerable policy efforts already embarked upon provides the best chance for the continuation of the impressive economic performance achieved over the past three years.

Notes and References

1. Labour force survey results show total employment falling by 1 000 in the year to April 1989 and increasing by 30 000 in the following twelve-month period. The poor overall employment growth in 1989 was due to a large fall in the number of people working in the public sector.

2. In the absence of official data on profit margins, the residual derived by subtracting wages and salaries from net output (the operating surplus) is used as an indicator of profits. See OECD *Economic Outlook 48,* pp. 128-9. Rates of return on capital have also risen, although they remain well below the OECD average: see Table 16).

3. Changes in unit labour costs may be affected by changes in the composition of output, so that they are not a completely accurate indicator of changes in competitiveness. Relative wage rates are an alternative indicator *(Diagram 6, panel C),* but these may understate competitive gains because of differences in productivity growth.

4. The surplus in high-tech trade does not measure the contribution of the high-tech sector to the trade balance, which depends on the amount of intra-industry trade (imports of parts etc) which may be quite high. In measuring the contribution of the high-tech sector to the current account balance, profit repatriation also has to be taken into account.

5. *Business and Finance,* 29th November 1990, pp. 12-13.

6. Housing starts were buoyant in the first quarter of 1990 and lower thereafter; for the year as a whole starts seem to have been about the same as in 1989.

7. The agreement is for pay increases not to exceed 4 per cent in 1991, 3 per cent in 1992 and 3³/₄ per cent in 1993, with higher increases for the lower paid and flexibility to negotiate an additional, discretionary increase of up to 3 per cent for the whole period of the Programme, on the basis of local criteria. The local bargaining element cannot come into effect before 1992 in the private sector, or before 1993 in the public sector.

8. For a discussion of the consistency problems which may arise between monetary and fiscal policies see "Medium-term Financial Strategy: the Co-ordination of

Fiscal and Monetary Policies", *OECD Economic Studies,* Spring 1984, which provides the background to the widespread adoption of tight money and fiscal policies among OECD economies in the 1980s. In principle, monetary restraint alone may be sufficient to engineer low and stable inflation, but higher interest rates exacerbate budget deficit problems and may undermine the longer-run credibility of a disinflation policy.

9. Under the ERM, (narrow band) deviations of up to 2.25 per cent are allowed from the fixed bilateral central rates *vis-à-vis* other member countries.

10. The German introduction of a 10 per cent withholding tax on investment earnings on 1st January 1989, followed by its abolition in July 1989, also caused substantial fluctuations in the flow of capital.

11. The central bank influences domestic interest rates through liquidity management instruments, such as sale and repurchase agreements, foreign exchange swaps and the short-term facility rate for banks.

12. Income tax receipts grew more slowly than total output, despite the substantial extra revenues from the tax amnesty in 1988. The tax amnesty was a one-off measure designed to encourage payment of tax arrears. About Ir£500 million was collected (compared to expected receipts of Ir£30 million), some of it probably representing a bringing forward of tax which would have been collected in 1989 as tax arrears.

13. Indirect taxes were the most buoyant revenue item. Car sales rose by 25 per cent and property and stock market activity also made a strong contribution. Income tax receipts were boosted by higher DIRT yields, due to higher interest rates, and by one-off improvements in collection arrangements, which accelerated PAYE payments.

14. The conditions required for the debt/GDP ratio to stabilise have been described in previous *OECD Surveys of Ireland.* They are that the non-interest surplus (generally known as the *primary* surplus) should be large enough to offset the increase in the debt/GNP ratio due to interest payments on debt. A formal description of this condition, which was given on pp. 102-3 of the 1987 *Survey,* can be derived from the equality $\Delta d = (r-g)d_0 - p$, where Δd is the change in the public debt/GNP ratio *(D/GNP)*; p is the primary (non-interest) balance; $r =$ the average interest rate on outstanding debt; and $g =$ the nominal growth of GNP, and $d =$ the debt/GNP ratio. If $\Delta d = 0$, $p = (r-g)d_0$. In the Diagram, values of the primary budget surplus consistent with stability of the debt/GNP ratio are compared with values of the actual primary surplus; the difference between the two is equivalent to the change in the debt ratio. In practice, for the purposes of calculation over discrete time periods $\Delta d = (r-g)d_0 /(1+g) - p$.

15. It is important to note that the effective interest rate on debt includes the effects of revaluation of foreign debt and of domestic bonds due to a discount from face

value, and these effects are taken into account in Diagram 14 and Table 17 below.

16. Inflation causes a reduction in the real value of outstanding fixed-interest government debt, which can be interpreted as an "inflation tax". The equality $\Delta d = (r-g)d_0 - p$, described above can be further decomposed to show a real interest rate and a real growth component: $\Delta d = \{(r-\pi)d_0 - \theta \, d_0\} - p$, where nominal income growth, g, is separated into an inflation component π and a real growth component θ. The first term in the square brackets $(r-\pi)d_0$ is an estimate of the effect of the real interest rate on the level of outstanding debt. If the rate of inflation exceeds the nominal interest rate $(r < \pi)$, debt holders suffer an implicit wealth tax as a result of unanticipated inflation; as inflation falls and/or debt is refinanced at rates which incorporate correct inflation expectations, the ability to impose such a wealth tax disappears. More orthodox revenue sources have then to be substituted to prevent the debt/GNP ratio increasing.

17. *Budget 1990*, p. 15.

18. See OECD *Economic Outlook 48*, p. 11.

19. A 1 percentage point rise in interest rates increases government spending by just over 3 per cent (i.e. 1 per cent of GNP).

20. In 1990 Swiss franc debt increased from 17.7 per cent of the total to 22 per cent. Deutschemark debt decreased slightly, from 37 per cent to 35.9 per cent reflecting the rise in German interest rates. Yen debt fell from 10.5 to 7.6 per cent.

21. Evidence on the extent to which government debt affects interest rates is, in some respects, ambiguous. Cross-section econometric work suggests a strong link between the budget *deficit* and interest rates (See OECD, *Economies in Transition,* p. 198), and the decline in the Irish interest rate differential with Germany in recent years appears to have been closely correlated with a lower EBR *(Diagram 12).* While there is also cross-section evidence that the level of government debt may be a factor determining interest rate differentials among OECD economies, in the Irish case, the correlation between the debt ratio and the interest rate differential is less strong. However, the higher the proportion of public debt in national wealth, the more the portfolio preferences of savers are likely to be disturbed and the greater the yields they will demand to hold such debt.

22. The baseline assumption is that the tax system will be indexed, so that pre- and post-tax incomes grow in parallel.

23. The proportion varies from 13 to 25 per cent depending on the type of bank. However, these ratios will be amended at the end of the year and the primary ratio was reduced from 10 to 8 per cent with effect from 20th March 1991. There are also prudential limitations on banks' overall open foreign exchange positions.

24. See NESC, *op. cit.,* p. 57.

25. See also the *1984/1985 OECD Economic Survey of Ireland* which contains a special chapter on industrial policy since the late 1950s.

26. The government has announced the intention of reducing its stake in Irish Life plc., from 90 to 34 per cent.

27. See pp. 89-91. A noteworthy feature is that minimum wages are fixed separately by Joint Labour Committees (JLCs) for fourteen categories of workers, taking account of the trading conditions in each sector. Some of the inflexibilities commonly associated with a uniform minimum wage are thus avoided.

28. There is some cross-country evidence that wage flexibility is related to the concentration of the wage-bargaining system in a bell-shaped way, implying that either very-centralised or very decentralised system are the most flexible. See *OECD Economies in Transition* and *OECD Economic Survey of Iceland, 1989/1990*, pp. 51-54.

29. The Council were of the opinion that "tax reform may now be the most powerful instrument available to the government to promote faster growth in output and employment in the short to medium term"; see *NESC, No. 83*, p. 822.

30. Because of interest payments on foreign debt and repatriated profits, national income (or GNP) is significantly lower than GDP in Ireland.

31. See, for example, *OECD, Economies in Transition, op. cit.*, pp. 168 *etseq.*, and *OECD Economic Survey of Canada*, pp. 63-4.

32. The Commission identified equity as the "first and most important consideration" among the three objectives of equity, efficiency and simplicity on which its review of the tax system was centred.

33. NESC., *A Strategy for the Nineties: Economic Stability and Structural Change,* October 1990, p. 6.36.

34. This system exists in Scandinavian countries, and is in the course of being introduced in the Netherlands.

35. The existence of a general exemption limit for income tax, designed to keep low income earners out of the tax net, involves a high marginal rate for low-paid tax payers with incomes not greatly in excess of the exemption limit. As income exceeds the exemption limit, a bridging rate of 53 per cent (52 per cent in 1991/92) is applied to the excess. This system only applies where it produces a lower tax bill (and hence a lower average tax rate) for the individual than taxation under the normal basis of allowances and reliefs.

36. The most notable exemptions are: government securities; life insurance policies; principal private residences and gains accruing to superannuation funds, charities and certain bodies such as local authorities and trade unions.

37. 100 per cent accelerated depreciation *plus* interest deductibility constitutes the equivalent of an interest-free loan.

38. 100 per cent accelerated depreciation allowances for plant, machinery and industrial buildings continue, however, to be available for certified service companies in Shannon and in the International Financial Services Centre, and for commercial buildings in "designated urban renewal areas".

39. The special 10 per cent rate for manufacturing was originally due to expire in the year 2000. The special rate is also available for Shannon service companies and companies in the International Financial Services Centre for whom it is due to expire in 2005.

40. In addition to benefiting from the special 10 per cent profit tax rate, such companies are exempt from withholding taxes on interest paid to foreign creditors and are eligible for continued 100 per cent accelerated capital depreciation allowances.

41. This has resulted in a considerable loss to the Exchequer and measures have been taken to limit the loans made under this provision (see *Table 26*).

42. The ability to do so is restricted to the year in which the losses arise. Losses sustained by companies whose trading income is taxed at an effective rate of 10 per cent may only be offset against income qualifying to be taxed at that rate.

43. Incentives include capital allowances for commercial building (allowed against income or corporation tax liabilities) and an entitlement to traders leasing refurbished buildings to set off double the rent as an allowance against trading income for ten years. This is twice the normal rate of set-off.

44. However, for a company taxed at the standard rate, incorporation can lead to a higher tax bill when both income and corporation taxes are taken into account.

45. Frank Cassels, "Company Taxation - a Crisis of Identity", in *The Taxation of Companies,* Foundation for Fiscal Studies, November 1989, p. 40.

46. *Ibid,* p. 38.

47. Under the partial imputation system the normal tax credit in 1990/91 was 28/72nds of the net distribution, which with a corporation tax rate of 43 per cent is equivalent to imputing 51.5 per cent of corporation tax to the shareholder $(28/72 \times ((1-.43)/.43))$. With a 40 per cent corporate profit tax rate the rate of imputation in 1991 will be $25/75 \times (1-.4)/.4 = 50$ per cent exactly. Since 1986, an individual shareholder in receipt of 10 per cent dividends is also entitled to a special relief, whereby half his dividends receipts are exempt from income tax, up to a limit.

48. While the number of statutory rates has been increased in 1991 from three to four, this does not signal a return to the multi-rate system which applied pre-1985; it can be regarded as a necessary transitional adjustment towards a harmonised EC VAT structure.

49. See *The Personal Income Tax Base, a Comparative Survey,* OECD, Paris, 1990. However, since the tax base relates only to PAYE income, such international comparisons are inconclusive.

50. See for example, *The Impact of Income Tax Reduction on Exchequer Revenue and the Economy,* Proceedings of the Third Annual Conference of the Foundation of Fiscal Studies, November 1988.

51. See NESC, *op. cit,* p. 208 *et seq.*

52. "Marginal Tax Rates on the use of Labour and Capital", *OECD Economic Studies,* Autumn 1986, p. 70.

53. See *OECD Economic Survey of Ireland 1988/89,* pp. 45 *et seq.*

54. F. Ruane and A. John, "Government Intervention and the Cost of Capital to Irish Manufacturing Industry", *The Economic and Social Review,* vol.16, No.1, October 1984, pp. 32.

55. See *OECD Economic Studies No. 7,* Autumn 1986, pp. 76 *et seq.*

56. However, in practice, contracting out from the manufacturing sector has

57. occurred widely in recent years in areas such as security, cleaning and other business services.

58. First Report of the Commission on Taxation, July 1982, p. 31.

59. The Capital Gains Tax, uncharacteristically, was levied only on real gains from 1978 onwards.

60. *Ibid,* pp. 2 *et seq.* The personal sector has shown an increasing preference for indirect holdings of marketable debt, including equities. Such indirect investment has significant advantages for individuals subject to high marginal tax rates in the case of dividend income. However, there is a disadvantage with respect to capital gains.

61. Rodney Thom, "The Taxation of Savings", *Foundation for Fiscal Studies, Research Report No.2,* October 1988.

62. Whether lump-sum retirement (or other pension benefit) should be included in the tax base depends on the tax treatment of preceding contributions and fund earnings. Various methods of maintaining neutrality are possible.

63. The remaining life assurance relief costs about Ir£9 million and approximately a further Ir£30 million could be raised by imposing a tax on lump-sum retirement benefits.

64. In Australia the Fringe Benefit Tax is imposed on employers at the top marginal rate of income tax and is not allowed as a deductible expense. Taxing fringe benefits at the employee level is more difficult.

65. Less than Ir£5 million of the total cost of exempting short-term benefits goes to the bottom three income deciles (which include less than ten per cent of those

affected). See T. Callan, *Income Tax Reform: a Microsimulation Approach,* Economic and Social Research Institute, March 1990.

66. A revenue-neutral package based on a single higher rate of 50 per cent would require a standard rate of 35 per cent.

67. The ability to move from one jurisdiction to another is the basis of the "Tiebout effect", whereby local taxes (particularly property taxes) and services do help determine the tax base.

68. D. de Buitleir, *Tax Reform in the 1990's,* Dublin Economics Workshop in Kenmare, 19th-21st October 1990, *mimeo.* Rates were abolished on residential property in 1978, and the calculation is based on the restoration of such a tax yielding aggregate revenue at the same ratio of GNP as before 1978.

69. See Callan, *op. cit.* Over 60 per cent of the value of tax expenditures on these reliefs goes to the top two income deciles.

70. Alternatively, it could be argued that the point of comparison should be the average marginal rate of dividend recipients. If the standard rate were used, the increase in the rate of imputation would be 71 per cent (a tax credit of two-thirds of the net dividend). See D. de Buitleir, *op. cit.*

Annex I

Technical notes and tables

Contributions to price changes (Diagram 4)

The decomposition of the domestic demand deflator is based on the following identity equations of expenditure and distribution:

$$P_G \equiv GNP/GNPV = (D + E - M)/GNPV$$
$$= P_D (DV/GNPV) + P_E (EV/GNPV) - P_M (MV/GNPV) \qquad [1]$$
$$P_G \equiv (W+Q+T)/GNPV = ULC + UQ + UT \qquad [2]$$

where the suffix V denotes volume and:

GNP = Gross National Product
W = total compensation of employees
T = net indirect taxes
Q = gross non-wage factor income ("profits"), defined as GDP minus (W+T)
D = total domestic demand
E = exports of goods and services, N.A. basis
M = imports of goods and services, N.A. basis
ULC = W/GNPV
UQ = Q/GNPV
UT = T/GNPV
P_G = GNP deflator
P_D = total domestic demand deflator
P_E = export deflator
P_M = import deflator

From [1] and [2], the following identity is derived:

$$\dot{P}_D = U\dot{L}C \left[\frac{GNPV}{DV} \right] + \dot{U}Q \left[\frac{GNPV}{DV} \right] + U\dot{T} \left[\frac{GNPV}{DV} \right] - \left[\dot{P}_E \frac{EV}{DV} - \dot{P}_M \frac{MV}{DV} \right] + R$$

where the dots above the variables represent growth rates (in per cent). The various components of changes in the domestic demand deflator are defined as changes in unit labour costs, unit profits, unit tax and terms-of-trade effects, respectively: R indicates effects of compositional changes.

Long-term interest rate differential *vis-à-vis* Germany (Diagram 12)

The Irish interest rate differential *vis-à-vis* Germany is specified as a function of the consumer price inflation differential between the two countries and the Irish exchequer borrowing requirement:

$$R_I - R_G = a_0 + a_1(PC_I - PC_G) + a_2D$$

where:

R_I = Irish government bond (seven years) yield
R_G = German government bond (ten years) yield
PC_I = Irish consumer price index, annual per cent increase
PC_G = German consumer price index, annual per cent increase
D = Ratio of the exchequer borrowing requirement to GNP

OLS estimates over the period 1976 to 1990 (annual data) yielded the following results:

Estimated coefficients (t-statistics)			Regression statistics		
a_0	a_1	a_2	SEE	DW	R^2
1.35 (3.0)	0.11 (2.3)	0.32 (2.9)	0.66	1.98	0.89

These results may be subject to simultaneity bias, since interest rates also affect the deficit. However, such a bias is likely to be small to the extent that *a)* the *differential* has often moved in a different direction from interest rates; and *b)* the effects of higher rates on the deficit come through with a lag. The existence of a strong contemporaneous link between the deficit and interest rates suggests that the deficit affects the interest rate differential significantly via expectations and "confidence effects".

The tax wedge (Diagram 21)

It was noted in the text that increased taxes have created a "wedge" between the employer's labour costs and the net wages received by the employee. The calculations are based on the average weekly earnings of adult male industrial workers; these are converted to annual income and rounded to the nearest Ir£50. Average and marginal tax rates are applied to the annual income for two types of household – a single person and a married couple with two dependent children. These rates (see Table A6) include social insurance charges, the Youth Employment Levy and (where applicable) the 1 per cent special levy on income. The household (a married couple with two dependent children, spouse not working) used in this calculation is assumed to have no other income, and no allowances other than the standard personal and dependents' allowances have been assumed.

Total labour costs per employee (the "product wage") are computed as gross wage income plus social security taxes paid by the employer. The "real product wage" is obtained by deflating labour cost per employee by the manufacturing output price index. To obtain the real product wage excluding payroll taxes, employees PRSI (Pay-Related Social Insurance) is deducted from the gross income, which is then deflated by the same price index. Real gross income excluding income taxes is derived using a constant-tax price index (which means excluding the effect of changes in indirect taxation from the consumer price index). Finally, the "real consumption wage" is defined as the gross income excluding both payroll taxes and income taxes deflated by the CPI, which includes the effect of indirect taxes. The difference between the real gross income excluding income taxes and "real consumption wage" measures the effect of indirect taxes.

The "low income trap" (Diagram 20)

The estimates of the "low income trap" i.e. the (gross) income range, in which increases in gross income lead to lower net income, are based on the following data:

The low income trap: man, wife, four children, 1989/1990

Ir£ per annum

Gross pay	Tax	PRSI	Levies	Net pay	Plus FIS	Medical card value	Net income	Less: LA rent	Travel to work costs	Net disposable income
3 000		165		2 835	2 184	440	5 459	94	520	4 845
4 000		220		3 780	2 184	440	6 404	140	520	5 744
5 000		275		4 725	2 184	440	7 349	187	520	6 642
6 000		330		5 670	2 184	440	8 294	681	529	7 093
7 000	120	385		6 495	1 560	440	8 495	910	520	7 065
7 875	645	433		6 797	1 040	440	8 277	952	520	6 805
8 000	720	440	180	6 660	988		7 648	936	520	6 197
9 000	1 220	495	203	7 082	364		7 446	993	520	5 930
10 000	1 540	550	225	7 685			7 685	1 082	520	6 083
10 500	1 700	578	236	7 986			7 986	1 123	520	6 340
11 000	1 860	605	248	8 287			8 287	1 165	520	6 602
12 000	2 180	660	270	8 890			8 890	1 456	520	6 914
13 000	2 500	715	293	9 492			9 492	1 555	520	7 417
14 000	2 820	770	315	10 095			10 095	1 659	520	7 916
15 000	3 140	825	338	10 697			10 697	1 758	520	8 419

Source: Department of Finance.

It will be noted that, but for the withdrawal of Family Income Supplement (FIS) as income rises, net disposable income would increase slightly as gross income rose from Ir£7 000 to Ir£9 000. FIS is currently paid to approximately 6 000 families, of which some 4 000 have gross pay below Ir£7 000. Hence some 2 000 earners only (with families of all sizes) are within the critical gross pay range – less than 0.2 per cent of total employment. However, the incentives facing families with gross incomes below Ir£7 000 will also be affected.

Effective tax rates on gross dividends and retentions (Table 31)

The effective tax rate calculations in Table 31 are based on the following definitions.

Corporation tax is paid on a unit of income at a rate t_c. Capital gains tax is assumed not payable on the proportion (θ) of corporate income which is retained[1], but income tax is charged at the shareholder's marginal rate t_y on net distributed profits $(1-\theta)(1-t_c)$, less a tax credit (cr), expressed as a proportion of the net dividend paid. The effective tax rate on corporate income is then:

$$ETR = t_c + (1-\theta)(1-t_c)[t_y - cr(1-t_y)]$$

The table illustrates the case of a corporation tax rate of 43 per cent, with a standard income tax rate of 35 per cent and a top rate of 58 per cent (the system operative in 1988/89). With a tax credit of 28/72 and $\theta = 0$ (all profits are distributed) the ETR would have reached a maximum of 66.8 per cent – giving a 23.8 per cent advantage to retained earnings for a top-rate taxpayer. Assuming the corporation tax rate is reduced to 40 per cent, the standard rate of income tax to 25 per cent and the top income tax rate to 50 per cent, with a rate of imputation of 25/75, the maximum ETR would fall to 60 per cent, with that applicable to a standard-rate payer falling to 40 per cent. This would still entail a substantial tax wedge in favour of retaining earnings for income earners subject to the top marginal rate, although it would eliminate the wedge for the standard-rate taxpayer.

Note

1. Capital gains arising on the disposal of an asset are taxed after adjustment for inflation, at rates of between 30 and 50 per cent, depending on the period of ownership. The first Ir£2 000 of net gains are tax free. In addition, capital gains are not subject to tax in the case of life assurance policies, superannuation funds, charities, and certain bodies such as local authorities and trade unions.

Table A1. **Foreign companies in the Irish economy**

Net output, wages and employment in 1987

	Total employment		Net output		Wages as per cent of net output
	Persons (1 000)	Per cent	Ir£ million	Per cent	
Total manufacturing	183.1	(100.0)	6 487.0	(100.0)	**31.2**
Irish	104.6	(57.2)	2 269.6	(35.0)	**47.0**
Foreign	78.4	(42.8)	4 217.4	(65.0)	**22.7**
Of which:					
EEC	29.6	(16.2)	958.5	(14.8)	**36.2**
Non-EEC	48.8	(26.6)	3 258.9	(50.2)	**18.8**
					(Foreign companies' share of net output) %
Foreign manufacturing by industry group					
Office and data processing equipment	5.9	(3.2)	822.9	(12.7)	**9.9** (99.6)
Pharmaceuticals	4.3	(2.3)	598.9	(9.2)	**11.6** (97.6)
Electrical engineering	14.5	(7.9)	601.5	(9.3)	**25.7** (90.3)
Instrument engineering	6.4	(3.5)	244.2	(3.8)	**29.4** (97.0)
Other food	2.6	(1.4)	556.4	(8.6)	**6.6** (89.8)

Source: CSO, Tables 5, 9 of the *Census of Industrial Production 1987.*

Table A2. **Irish merchandise trade by area**

Percentage

| | A. Exports | | | |
	United Kingdom	EEC excluding United Kingdom	United States	Others
1960	74.8	7.4	7.5	10.3
1970	66.3	12.7	10.0	11.0
1980	43.2	32.1	5.3	19.4
1987	34.2	39.3	7.8	18.7
1988	35.4	38.6	7.7	18.3
1989	33.5	40.7	7.9	17.9
1990	33.7	41.1	8.2	17.0
	B. Imports			
1960	49.6	14.4	8.3	27.7
1970	53.5	18.8	7.0	20.7
1980	50.8	20.1	8.7	20.4
1987	41.7	23.9	17.0	17.4
1988	42.1	23.9	15.9	18.1
1989	40.9	24.5	16.1	18.5
1990	42.2	24.4	14.6	18.8

Source: Trade Statistics of Ireland.

Table A3. Public sector employment

	Exchequer finances	Local authorities	Commercial semi-state bodies	Total public sector 000s	Total public sector Per cent change
		Per cent change			
1978-82	15.0	3.7	11.2		13.9
1982-90	−9.6	−18.7	−22.6		−14.4
		In 000s			
1982	188.8	32.6	92.9	314.3	3.4
1983	188.1	33.0	91.4	312.5	−0.6
1984	186.6	32.5	88.2	307.3	−1.7
1985	184.9	32.6	85.1	302.6	−1.5
1986	185.5	32.8	82.4	300.7	−0.6
1987	184.7	32.4	78.4	295.5	−1.7
1988	179.6	30.3	75.8	285.7	−3.3
1989	170.8	27.4	71.9	270.1	−5.5
1990	170.7	26.5	71.9	269.1	−0.4

Source: Department of Finance. Figures after 1982 are for full-time equivalents, they contain an element of estimation.

Table A4. Pay comparisons for the government sector

	Average real pay index (1977=100)	Average pay of government sector employees Ir£	Average pay of government sector employees Per cent increase	Government employees	Clerical Assistant[1]	Higher Executive Officer[1]	School Teacher[1]
				As per cent of average industrial earnings			
1975	103	3 100	–	113			
1976	103	3 670	18.4	111			
1977	100	4 030	9.8	105			
1978	109	4 730	28.9	108	51	127	96
1979	116	5 710	20.7	114	54	130	98
1980	128	7 929	38.9	134	51	121	92
1981	125	9 335	17.7	136	60	136	106
1982	119	10 458	12.0	137	60	131	106
1983	120	11 631	11.2	136	59	130	105
1984	120	11 750	10.2	122	55	123	97
1985	121	12 527	6.6	119	53	121	94
1986	123	13 421	7.1	119	49	113	87
1987	127	14 178	5.6	120	49	113	90
1988	127	14 478	2.1	117	49	113	92
1989	133	15 714	8.5	122	49	111	94
1990	140	17 054	8.5	127	49	115	93

1. Pay scales in force on 1st January each year. The pay given is the minimum on the scale (honours degree assumed for teacher).
Note: The average real pay index, affected as it is by special factors which can change sharply from year to year, should be interpreted as indicating only broad trends. Average industrial earnings as shown in Table A7.
Source: Department of Finance and OECD.

Table A5. **Average transfer payments**[1]

	Old age (contributory pensions)[2]		Unemployment benefits[3]		*Memorandum:* Average real per capita consumption
	Nominal	Real	Nominal	Real	
1976	15.55	100.0	18.28	100.0	100.0
1977	17.81	100.8	20.79	100.9	105.3
1978	20.75	109.2	23.97	107.3	113.4
1979	23.70	110.1	28.16	111.3	116.5
1980	31.10	122.3	35.69	119.3	115.9
1981	38.55	125.8	43.70	121.3	116.4
1982	49.08	136.7	52.39	124.2	107.1
1983	54.54	137.6	55.12	118.4	107.2
1984	58.79	136.6	56.18	111.1	108.6
1985	62.33	137.4	59.98	112.5	112.1
1986	64.96	137.8	60.48	109.2	114.4
1987	66.97	137.7	60.65	106.1	116.9
1988	68.75	138.2	59.03	101.4	119.9
1989	70.72	137.1	59.64	98.5	126.9
1990	73.87	138.2	60.58	96.7	–

1. Average weekly payments are given throughout in Irish pounds.
2. Total disbursements divided by the number of recipients. Other pensions (i.e. non-contributory and widows and orphans) moved in a similar way.
3. Unemployment plus pay-related benefits divided by the number of unemployment benefit recipients.
Source: Department of Finance.

Table A6. Average and marginal tax rates on labour income and unemployment benefits

			Single employee		Married employee with 2 children								Memorandum:
			Tax rates per cent[1]		Tax rates per cent[1]			Unemployment benefits				
								Short-term[2]		Annual[3]		
	Average income (real) (1980=100)	Average annual income Ir£	Average	Marginal	Average	Marginal	Net income after tax Ir£	Average Ir£	Replacement ratio[4]	Average Ir£	Replacement ratio[4]	Average weekly earnings, male adult Ir£
1980	100	5 900	28.8	39.5	17.2	39.5	4 886	3 978.2	81.4	3 608.8	73.9	113.11
1981	96.4	6 850	29.5	39.75	20.4	39.75	5 454	4 537.0	83.2	4 280.2	78.5	131.55
1982	92.0	7 650	32.1	52.5	21.5	42.5	6 003	5 206.2	86.7	5 003.9	83.1	147.52
1983	93.2	8 550	35.6	63.5	24.8	43.5	6 426	5 257.2	81.8	5 018.9	78.1	164.58
1984	96.4	9 600	37.7	63.5	26.4	43.5	7 064	5 656.6	80.1	5 424.2	76.8	184.40
1985	100.1	10 500	38.7	68.5	27.2	43.5	7 643	6 074.1	79.5	5 829.9	76.3	201.98
1986	103.2	11 250	38.0	65.5	27.0	42.5	8 214	6 356.0	77.4	6 124.6	74.6	216.66
1987	104.9	11 800	39.5	65.75	28.0	42.75	8 501	5 638.9	66.3	6 458.0	75.9	227.30
1988	107.3	12 350	38.1	65.75	28.1	42.75	8 885	5 797.0	65.2	5 797.0	65.2	237.69
1989	107.7	12 900	36.9	63.75	26.9	39.75	9 432	5 923.8	62.8	5 923.8	62.8	247.86
1989[5]	–	20 650	–	–	31.7	55.75	14 100	7 219.2	51.2	7 219.2	51.2	

Note: Revised industrial earnings data are available from 1985 and these have been used in this table.
1. Including employee social security contributions.
2. Unemployment benefit plus pay-related benefits at the initial maximum rate of average male industrial worker (excluding income tax rebates).
3. Annual entitlement to unemployment benefit plus pay-related benefits for the average male industrial worker (excluding income tax rebates) at assumed maximum rates. This calculation takes account of the fact that until 1987 pay-related benefit declined during the course of the year.
4. Unemployment benefits divided by net income after tax, per cent.
5. Tax and benefit position when the spouse also works and earns 60 per cent of the principal earner's income.
Sources: Department of Finance; Secretariat calculations.

Table A7. Costs of Exchequer borrowing

Ir£ million

	Debt		Exchequer borrowing requirement	Revaluation effects due to			Effective interest rate[2] [B]	Total cost	
	End year level	(Per cent of GNP)[2]		[1] Exchange rate changes	[2] Domestic discounting[1]	[1]+[2] as per cent of debt[2] [A]		As per cent of debt (=[A]+[B])	Ir£ million
1983	14 392	105.9	1 756	858	108	7.4	10.2	17.6	2 296
1984	16 821	113.7	1 825	362	243	3.9	10.0	13.9	2 171
1985	18 502	117.9	2 015	−602	268	−1.9	10.3	8.5	1 493
1986	21 611	129.2	2 145	294	670	4.8	9.1	13.9	2 781
1987	23 694	131.0	1 786	−119	416	1.3	8.5	9.9	2 232
1988	24 611	129.9	619[3]	248	52	1.2	8.1	9.4	2 262
1989	24 828	118.9	479	−346	27	−1.3	7.9	6.6	1 637
1990[4]	25 110	111.1	462	−180	45	−0.5	8.4	7.9	1 984

Note: The calculations underlying this table are approximate only.
1. Includes some other minor elements.
2. Calculated as a percentage of the average debt outstanding in the year.
3. If the exceptional once-off receipts from the tax amnesty are excluded, the underlying EBR figure for 1988 was Ir£1 119 million.
4. Provisional outturns.
Sources: Finance Accounts (Stationery Office, Dublin); Department of Finance.

113

Annex II

Chronology of main economic events and policy measures

1989

30th June 1989

The Central Bank increases the key short-term facility rate by 1 percentage point to 10 per cent.

5th July

The Central Bank Bill 1988 is passed by the Seanad (Upper House).

12th July

The Central Bank Bill 1988 (now known as the Central Bank Act, 1989) becomes law with the exception of certain sections which have phased implementation dates of 1st September and 1st November. The Building Societies Bill 1988 (now the Building Societies Act, 1989) is enacted and the Central Bank assumes responsibility for supervision of Building Societies from 1st September 1989.

27th September

Community Support Framework adopted by EC Commission for the period 1st January 1989 to 31st December 1993. ECU 1 646 million from the Social Fund is committed to Ireland (1989 prices). ERDF assistance of ECU 1 372 million is also made available, plus ECU 654 million under FEOGA.

6th October

The Central Bank raises the short-term facility rate by 1 percentage point to 11 per cent.

8th December

The short-term facility rate is raised for the fourth time in 1989 by 1 percentage point to 12 per cent.

23rd December

The Trustee Savings Bank Bill 1989 is passed. The Bill:
- Provides for the licensing and supervision of such banks by the Central Bank;
- Enables the Minister of Finance to authorise their reorganisation into companies.

1990

31st January

The Minister of Finance introduces the Budget for 1990.

It provides for a current budget deficit of Ir£257 million or 1.2 per cent of GNP and for an Exchequer Borrowing requirement of Ir£449 million or 2.1 per cent of GNP.

A new medium-term objective for public finances is announced involving the reduction of the National Debt/GNP ratio towards 100 per cent by 1993 and achieving balance on the current budget.

Welfare payments and health allowances increased by 5 per cent, from July, – with higher increases for certain beneficiaries. Adjustments in income tax rates, allowances and bands equivalent to a Ir£106 million reduction in revenue.

Changes in tax and social insurance systems to benefit low income earners:
- The standard income tax rate is to be reduced from 32 per cent to 30 per cent. The top rate is to be reduced from 56 per cent to 53 per cent;
- The standard rate of VAT is to be reduced from 25 per cent to 23 per cent.

First year accelerated capital depreciation allowances against corporation tax reduced from 50 per cent to 25 per cent on investment made from 1st April 1991, and it is announced that they will be eliminated after 31st March 1992. The standard rate of corporation tax to be reduced from 43 per cent to 40 per cent from 1st April 1991.

The top rate of capital gains tax is reduced from 60 per cent to 50 per cent.

Ir£20.1 million provided to implement National Environment Action Plan (expenditure and taxation measures).

The third phase of the programme to eliminate exchange controls is implemented. This further reduces administrative requirements and permits greater access to some of the innovative financial instruments like swaps, futures and options.

1st June

For the first time in two years the Central Bank lowers the short-term facility rate by 0.5 percentage points to 11.5 per cent.

27th June

The Central Bank lowers the short-term facility rate by 0.5 per cent to 11 per cent.

17th October

Opening of talks between Government, employers, trade unions and farming interests on a proposed Programme for Economic and Social Progress (to succeed the Programme for National Recovery).

19th October

The short-term facility rate is lowered for the third successive time by 0.5 percentage points to 10.5 per cent.

3rd December

The Minister of Finance signs an order under the National Treasury Management Act, 1990, establishing the National Treasury Agency with effect from 3rd December 1990. The Government delegates to the Agency, by order, the functions of borrowing money for the Exchequer, managing the National Debt and certain related matters. Previously these functions were undertaken in the Department of Finance.

20th December

The Minister of Finance announces the extension to 2005 of the 10 per cent rate of corporation tax for projects in the International Financial Services Centre in Dublin and the Shannon Customs-Free Airport zone.

21st December

The Central Bank raises the short-term facility rate by 0.75 percentage points to 11.25 per cent.

1991

14th January

Agreement is reached between Government and representatives of employers, trade unions and farmers on a Programme for Economic and Social Progress. Trade unions to consult their members on its terms by ballot.

30th January

The Minister of Finance introduces the Budget for 1991.

It provides for a current budget deficit of Ir£245 million or 1 per cent of GNP, and an Exchequer Borrowing requirement of Ir£460 or 1.9 per cent of GNP.

Welfare payments to be increased by 4 per cent, with higher increases for certain beneficiaries.

Social insurance cover extended to part-time workers. Adjustments in income tax allowances and rates equivalent to an Ir£53 million reduction in revenue in 1991.

The standard rate of income tax is reduced from 30 per cent to 29 per cent. The top rate is reduced from 53 per cent to 52 per cent.

The time limit for approvals for new firms setting up in the International Financial Services Centre is extended to end-1994. The 10 per cent corporation tax rate for companies in the Centre is extended to end-2005.

Self-assessment is extended to capital gains tax.

The standard rate of VAT reduced from 23 per cent to 21 per cent.

The 10 per cent VAT rate is increased to 12½ per cent, with the exception of building, hotel accommodation and some other minor items which remain liable at 10 per cent.

It is announced that the Irish Life Assurance Company will be floated on the stock market in 1991.

Road tax rates on motor vehicles are rationalised and increased by about 10 per cent on average.

20th February

Federated Irish Employers accept terms of Programme for Economic and Social Progress.

21st February

Irish Congress of Trade Unions accepts terms of Programme for Economic and Social Progress, by ballot.

STATISTICAL ANNEX

Selected background statistics

	Average 1981-1989	1981	1982	1983	1984	1985	1986	1987	1988	1989
A. Percentage changes from previous year										
Private consumption[1]	1.4	1.7	-7.1	0.9	2.0	3.5	2.0	2.2	2.4	5.2
Gross fixed capital formation[1]	-0.8	7.3	-3.3	-9.0	-2.7	-7.4	-1.3	-3.7	2.6	12.0
GNP[1]	1.5	2.6	-0.7	-1.6	2.3	1.0	-1.2	5.0	1.4	5.0
GNP price deflator	8.2	17.5	15.6	10.9	6.2	5.4	8.0	2.6	3.3	4.9
Industrial production	6.5	6.5	-1.9	8.1	9.6	3.4	2.2	8.9	10.7	11.6
Employment	-0.7	-0.9	0.2	-2.1	-1.8	-2.5	0.5	0.6	0.3	-0.1
Compensation of employees (current prices)	8.5	18.5	14.1	9.3	8.5	6.1	6.2	5.4	4.7	4.5
Productivity (GNP/employment)	2.2	3.5	-0.9	0.5	4.2	3.6	-1.6	4.3	1.2	5.1
Unit labour costs (Compensation/GNP)	6.9	15.5	14.9	11.1	6.1	5.1	7.5	0.4	3.2	-0.5
B. Percentage ratios										
Gross fixed capital formation as % of GNP at constant prices	22.9	27.5	26.7	24.7	23.5	21.5	21.5	19.7	20.0	21.3
Stockbuilding as % of GNP at constant prices	0.4	-0.9	1.3	0.7	1.4	1.1	0.8	0.1	-0.8	0.4
Foreign Balance as % of GNP at current prices	0.9	-10.4	-6.0	-3.4	0.0	2.2	0.4	6.1	9.9	9.8
Compensation of employees as % of GNP at current prices	59.8	61.1	60.7	60.8	60.7	60.5	60.2	58.9	58.9	55.8
Direct taxes as percent of household income	14.7	11.7	12.5	13.5	14.7	14.7	15.5	15.9	17.2	17.0
Household saving as percent of disposable income	16.7	16.8	20.3	18.8	18.2	16.1	15.6	17.4	14.7	12.0
Unemployment as percent of total labour force	15.0	9.9	11.4	14.0	15.5	17.4	17.4	17.5	16.7	15.6
C. Other indicator										
Current balance (billion dollars)	-0.7	-2.6	-1.9	-1.2	-1.0	-0.7	-0.7	0.4	0.7	0.5

1. At Constant 1985 prices.
Source: OECD Secretariat.

Table A. Expenditure on gross national product, current prices

Ir£ million

	1980	1981	1982	1983	1984	1985	1986	1987	1988	1989[1]
Private consumption	6 157.6	7 489.9	8 025.6	8 813.8	9 651.7	10 490.6	11 168.0	11 782.8	12 376	13 523
Public consumption	1 860.2	2 260.3	2 620.7	2 857.3	3 066.6	3 301.0	3 542.1	3 576.6	3 595	3 683
Gross fixed investment	2 718.4	3 350.4	3 531.0	3 414.4	3 505.7	3 388.7	3 423.0	3 337.8	3 627	4 320
Final domestic demand	10 736.2	13 100.6	14 177.3	15 085.5	16 224.0	17 180.3	18 133.1	18 697.2	19 598	21 526
	(18.9)	(22.0)	(8.2)	(6.4)	(7.5)	(5.9)	(5.5)	(3.1)	(4.8)	(9.8)
Stockbuilding	-114.2	-128.0	185.3	106.2	227.7	168.9	112.6	26.7	-83	90
	(-3.9)	(-0.2)	(2.9)	(-0.6)	(0.9)	(-0.4)	(-0.4)	(-0.5)	(-0.6)	(0.9)
Total domestic demand	10 622.0	12 972.6	14 362.6	15 191.7	16 451.7	17 349.2	18 245.7	18 723.9	19 515	21 616
	(15.3)	(22.1)	(10.7)	(5.8)	(8.3)	(5.5)	(5.2)	(2.6)	(4.2)	(10.8)
Exports	4 638.6	5 503.6	6 433.3	7 751.6	9 770.0	10 738.4	10 351.5	11 785.1	13 533	15 991
Imports	5 899.9	7 117.2	7 414.5	8 164.2	9 815.1	10 396.6	9 860.4	10 467.6	11 565	13 688
Foreign balance	-1261.3	-1613.6	-981.2	-412.6	-45.1	341.8	491.1	1 317.5	1 968	2 303
	(0.5)	(-3.9)	(-5.8)	(4.6)	(-2.7)	(2.6)	(0.9)	(4.9)	(3.6)	(1.8)
GDP(market prices)	9 360.7	11 359.0	13 381.4	14 779.1	16 406.6	17 691.0	18 736.8	20 041.4	21 483	23 919
Net factor income from abroad	-358.1	-504.6	-927.7	-1183.9	-1638.8	-1965.7	-1957.0	-1957.1	-2542	-3039
GNP(market prices)	9 002.6	10 854.4	12 453.7	13 595.2	14 767.8	15 725.3	16 779.8	18 084.3	18 941	20 880
	(17.9)	(20.6)	(14.7)	(9.2)	(8.6)	(6.5)	(6.7)	(7.8)	(4.7)	(10.2)
Memorandum:										
Composition of stockbuilding										
Agriculture	-151.7	-5.0	29.8	4.4	39.5	-23.9	-70.7	26.7	80	184
Non-agriculture (incl. EEC intervention stocks)	37.5	-123.0	155.5	101.8	188.2	192.8	183.3	0.0	-163	-94

1. Preliminary.

Note: Figures in parentheses are annual growth rates; for stockbuilding and the foreign balance they are contributions to growth rates.

Sources: CSO, *National Income and Expenditure;* Department of Finance, *Economic Review and Outlook;*; OECD estimates.

Table B. Expenditure on gross national product, constant 1985 prices

Ir£ million

	1980	1981	1982	1983	1984	1985	1986	1987	1988	1989[1]
Private consumption	10 419.8	10 596.8	9 848.9	9 932.8	10 132.4	10 490.6	10 705.6	10 944.9	11 213	11 792
Public consumption	3 163.1	3 173.6	3 276.6	3 264.6	3 241.9	3 301.0	3 383.7	3 218.9	3 084	2 976
Gross fixed investment	3 922.4	4 296.2	4 149.6	3 760.8	3 660.8	3 388.7	3 344.4	3 219.8	3 302	3 698
Final domestic demand	17 505.3	18 066.6	17 275.1	16 958.2	17 035.1	17 180.3	17 433.7	17 383.6	17 599	18 466
	(0.3)	(3.2)	(-4.4)	(-1.8)	(0.5)	(0.9)	(1.5)	(-0.3)	(1.2)	(4.9)
Stockbuilding	-149.4	-175.8	179.5	104.0	216.8	168.9	126.5	16.3	-127	61
	(-3.3)	(-0.2)	(2.3)	(-0.5)	(0.7)	(-0.3)	(-0.3)	(-0.7)	(-0.9)	(1.1)
Total domestic demand	17 355.9	17 890.8	17 454.6	17 062.2	17 251.9	17 349.2	17 560.2	17 399.9	17 472	18 527
	(-2.4)	(3.1)	(-2.4)	(-2.2)	(1.1)	(0.6)	(1.2)	(-0.9)	(0.4)	(6.0)
Exports	7 271.4	7 413.6	7 824.0	8 641.8	10 075.5	10 738.4	11 048.3	12 527.0	13 615	14 990
Imports	8 887.8	9 039.8	8 758.0	9 166.6	10 069.9	10 396.6	10 981.7	11 530.2	11 980	13 283
Foreign balance	-1 616.4	-1 626.2	-934.0	-524.8	5.6	341.8	66.6	997	1 635	1 707.0
	(5.8)	(-0.1)	(4.5)	(2.6)	(3.5)	(2.2)	(-1.8)	(6.0)	(3.9)	(0.4)
GDP (market prices)	15 686.2	16 207.8	16 577.9	16 537.4	17 257.5	17 691.0	17 626.8	18 396.7	19 107	20 234
Net factor income from abroad	-561.3	-679.5	-1 128.5	-1 319.9	-1 690.0	-1 965.7	-2 088.7	-2 080.3	-2 558	-2 849
GNP (market prices)	15 124.9	15 528.3	15 449.4	15 217.5	15 567.5	15 725.3	15 538.1	16 316.4	16 549	17 385
	(2.7)	(2.7)	(-0.5)	(-1.5)	(2.3)	(1.0)	(-1.2)	(5.0)	(1.4)	(5.1)
Memorandum :										
Composition of stockbuilding										
Agriculture			29.8	5.4	36.2	-23.9	-73.7	24.9	63	153
Non-agriculture (inlc. EEC intervention stocks)			149.7	98.7	180.6	192.8	200.2	-8.5	-190	-92

1. Preliminary.
Note: Figures in parentheses are annual growth rates; for stockbuilding and the foreign balance they are contributions to growth rates.
Sources: CSO, *National Income and Expenditure;* Department of Finance, *Economic Review and Outlook;* OECD estimates.

Table C. Agricultural output and income

Ir£ million

	1981	1982	1983	1984	1985	1986	1987	1988	1989	1990
Gross agricultural product [A]	1 986	2 280	2 555	2 836	2 739	2 721	2 873	3 159	3 358	3 170
Inputs [B]	919	1 011	1 140	1 219	1 262	1 288	1 176	1 224	1 342	1 372
Gross agricultural product[1] [C = A – B]	1 067	1 269	1 415	1 617	1 477	1 433	1 697	1 935	2 015	1 798
Other expenses less subsidies[2] [D]	282	287	284	270	258	290	304	282	288	156
INCOME (self-employed) [= C – D]	786	982	1 132	1 347	1 219	1 143	1 393	1 653	1 727	1 640
	(17.0)	(24.9)	(15.3)	(19.0)	(−9.5)	(−6.2)	(21.9)	(18.7)	(4.5)	(−5.0)
Volume changes:										
Gross agricultural output	−0.2	6.5	3.3	8.4	−1.5	−1.2	1.2	1.6	2.1	6.3
Inputs	5.6	−0.4	5.5	−0.4	1.4	6.3	−3.7	0.9	5.5	2.0
Gross agricultural product	−4.9	12.5	1.5	15.8	−3.4	−7.5	6.0	2.4	−1.2	10.4
Price changes										
Gross agricultural output	16.4	7.8	8.5	2.4	−2.0	0.6	4.3	8.2	4.2	−11.2
Inputs	14.5	10.5	6.9	7.5	2.2	−4.0	−5.2	3.2	3.9	0.2
Gross agricultural product	17.9	5.7	9.9	−1.3	−5.5	4.9	11.8	11.4	5.4	−19.2

1. At market prices. Gross agricultural product measures value added.
2. Depreciation plus wages and salaries plus land annuities plus agricultural levies less subsidies.
Note: Figures in parentheses are annual growth rates.
Sources: CSO, *Statistical Abstract.*

Table D. **Prices and wages**

	Units	1980	1981	1982	1983	1984	1985	1986	1987	1988	1989	1990
Agricultural prices	1985=100	73.7	86.8	94.0	99.9	102.8	100.0	99.5	103.5	114.4	120.1	106.4
Livestock price index	1985=100	72.5	87.7	95.1	99.2	102.6	100.0	95.6	101.2	113.8	112.4	100.1
Consumer prices	1985=100	56.1	67.6	79.2	87.4	94.9	100.0	103.9	107.2	109.5	113.9	117.8
Wholesale prices[1]	1985=100	63.9	74.6	82.9	88.3	97.1	100.0	97.8	98.4	102.4	108.1	–
Industrial prices[2]	1985=100	65.4	75.8	84.7	90.5	96.6	100.0	98.8	100.4	104.5	109.5	107.8
Average hourly earnings in manufacturing	1985=100	54.1	63.0	76.4	85.3	92.3	100.0	106.8	112.9	118.1	124.1	–

1. General wholesale price index.
2. Output of manufacturing industry.
Sources: CSO, *Statistical Bulletin*; OECD, *Main Economic Indicators*.

Table E. Household appropriation account

Ir£ million

	1980	1981	1982	1983	1984	1985	1986	1987	1988	1989[2]
Total personal income	8 821.0	10 828.1	12 329.4	13 522.9	14 917.4	15 830.8	16 895.3	18 282.1	18 998.0	20 046.0
of which:										
Agricultural	788.1	910.7	1 122.8	1 273.9	1 500.5	1 384.1	1 314.0	1 582.2	1 855.0	1 956.0
Non-agricultural employee compensation	5 491.7	6 522.1	7 446.6	8 163.0	8 857.9	9 396.5	9 983.3	10 519.9	11 015.0	11 709.0
Transfers	1 344.3	1 746.0	2 292.0	2 595.4	2 868.0	3 129.3	3 419.3	3 605.0	3 708.0	3 734.0
Direct taxation	1 486.2	1 829.2	2 272.5	2 665.1	3 123.2	3 331.9	3 625.1	3 998.5	4 463.0	4 300.0
(as percentage of income)	(16.8)	(16.9)	(18.4)	(19.7)	(20.9)	(21.0)	(21.5)	(21.9)	(23.5)	(21.5)
Personal disposable income	7 334.8	8 998.9	10 056.9	10 857.8	11 794.2	12 498.9	13 270.2	14 283.6	14 535.0	15 747.0
Savings ratio (percentage)	16.0	16.8	20.2	18.8	18.2	16.1	15.8	17.5	14.9	14.1
Personal consumption	6 157.6	7 489.9	8 025.6	8 813.8	9 651.7	10 490.6	11 168.0	11 782.8	12 376.0	13 523.0
Memorandum:										
Real disposable income[1]	12 412.1	12 732.0	12 341.8	12 236.6	12 381.1	12 499.4	12 721.2	13 268.0	13 175.1	13 741.7
(percentage change)	-1.8	2.6	-3.1	-0.9	1.2	1.0	1.8	4.3	-0.7	4.3

1. Deflated by personal consumption deflator.
2. Department of Finance estimates.
Source : CSO, *National Income and Expenditure.*

Table F. **Budgetary position**

Ir£ million

	1985		1986		1987		1988		1989		1990	
	January Estimate	Outturn[2]	Estimate	Outturn	Estimate	Outturn	Estimate	Outturn	Estimate	Outturn	Estimate	Outturn
Current budget:												
Expenditure	7 634	7 615	8 042	8 105	8 417	8 331	8 160	8 007	8 150	8 019	8 387	8 421
Revenue	6 400	6 331	6 792	6 710	7 217	7 151	7 035	7 690	7 331	7 756	8 130	8 269
Deficit	1 234	1 284	1 250	1 395	1 200	1 180	1 125	317	819	263	257	152
(as % of GNP)	7.9	8.2	7.5	8.3	6.6	6.5	6.0	1.7	3.9	1.3	1.2	0.7
Capital budget:												
Expenditure												
Public capital programme	1 806	1 693	1 681	1 646	1 655	1 576	1 376	1 337	1 392	1 414	1 670	1 661
Other	45	68	70	98	75	43	40	25	30	19	25	23
Total	1 851	1 761	1 751	1 744	1 730	1 619	1 416	1 362	1 422	1 433	1 695	1 684
Ressources	1 066	1 030	1 000	994	1 072	1 013	1 084	1 060	1 186	1 217	1 503	1 374
Deficit	785	731	751	750	658	506	332	302	236	216	192	310
Exchequer borrowing requirement	2 019	2 015	2 001	2 145	1 858	1 786	1 457	619	1 055	479	449	462
(as % of GNP)	12.9	12.8	12.0	12.8	10.3	9.9	7.8	3.3	5.1	2.3	2.1	2.0
Memorandum:												
Current Expenditure[1]	48.6	48.5	48.0	48.3	46.5	46.1	43.1	42.3	39.0	38.4	37.1	37.3
Current revenue[1]	40.7	40.3	40.5	40.0	40.0	39.5	37.1	40.6	35.1	37.1	36.0	36.6
Public capital programme[1]	11.5	10.8	10.0	9.8	9.2	8.7	7.3	7.1	6.7	6.8	7.4	7.3

1. As a percentage of GNP.
2. The 1985 Provisional Outturn figures for the Public Capital Programme have been adjusted in line with the 1986 reclassification of certain Bord Telecom Eireann Expenditure.

Sources: Budget documents; Department of Finance.

Table G. Public expenditure

Ir£ million

	1981	1982	1983	1984	1985	1986	1987	1988	1989¹	1990¹
Total public investment	1 650	1 858	1 709	1 734	1 695	1 647	1 565	1 335	1 391	1 653
(as % of GNP)	(15.2)	(15.0)	(12.6)	(11.8)	(10.8)	(9.8)	(8.7)	(7.0)	(6.7)	(7.3)
Sectoral economic investment	527	541	438	413	383	394	376	370	445	521
of which: IDA	(215)	(211)	(176)	(174)	(172)	(170)	(152)	(132)	(127)	(137)
Productive infrastructure	667	780	709	758	709	638	587	591	651	802
Social infrastructure	456	537	562	563	603	615	602	374	295	330
Central Government current spending	4 997	6 337	7 247	7 867	8 682	9 121	9 681	9 714	9 742	10 051
(as % of GNP)	(46.0)	(60.0)	(53.3)	(53.2)	(55.3)	(54.5)	(53.7)	(51.7)	(46.7)	(44.5)
National debt interest	823	1 179	1 343	1 518	1 798	1 742	1 886	1 977	2 040	2 139
of which: External	(266)	(526)	(597)	(720)	(795)	(761)	(804)	(894)	(973)	–
Current transfers	1 416	1 884	2 222	2 441	2 714	2 948	3 074	3 200	3 136	3 348
Expenditure on goods and services	1 172	1 378	1 576	1 702	1 818	1 974	2 054	2 023	2 073	2 245
Current grants to local authorities	1 156	1 405	1 679	1 787	1 937	2 017	2 089	1 799	1 838	1 995
Memorandum:										
Public capital programme (volume²; 1985=100)										
Sectoral economic investment	176	165	126	113	100	100	95	88	100	118
Productive infrastructure	120	129	110	112	100	88	80	76	79	98
of which:										
Roads, etc.	75	92	94	93	100	99	90	76	89	101
Social infrastructure	96	104	103	98	100	99	96	57	42	47
Total	124	128	111	107	100	95	89	72	71	84

1. Department of Finance estimates.
2. Deflator used is that for Gross Fixed Capital Formation.
Sources: Budget statements; CSO, *National Income and Expenditure*; Department of Finance, *Public Capital Programme,* 1991.

Table H. Government revenue

Ir£ million

	1981	1982	1983	1984	1985	1986	1987	1988	1989	1990[1]
Taxes on income and wealth	2 032.2	2 510	2 887	3 340	3 557	3 919	4 275	4 821	4 659	5 164
of which:										
Income taxes	1 246.1	1 458	1 661	1 968	2 105	2 383	2 718	3 048	2 831	3 024
Corporation taxes	199.7	232	215	210	218	258	256	335	303	477
Social insurance contributions	562.1	739	844	935	1 003	1 049	1 109	1 213	1 294	1 420
Employer	368.0	472	530	595	628	661	701	727	783	859
Employee	194.1	267	313	340	369	377	407	467	471	508
Self employed								22	46	52
Taxes on expenditure	1 742.5	2 158	2 465[1]	2 738	2 879	3 015	3 160	3 478	3 826	3 898
Other revenue	525.7	690	918[1]	889	1 043	931	1 051	522	612	651
Total income on current account	4 300.4	5 358	6 271[1]	6 967	7 479	7 875	8 486	9 016	9 097[3]	9 713[3]
(% of GNP)	(39.6)	(43.0)	(46.1)	(47.2)	(47.6)	(47.0)	(47.0)	(47.6)	(43.0)	(43.0)
Memorandum:										
Rates[2] paid to local authorities	109.8	103.9	115.6	136.0	153	167	184	194	228	240

1. Not adjusted to reflect the reclassification of accounts arising from the transfer, in 1984, of the day-to-day operations of the postal and telecommunications services from Central Government.
2. Rates are property taxes.
3. Provisional figure for 1989 and 1990.
Sources : Budget statements (various issues); CSO, *National Income and Expenditure.*

128

Table 1. Public sector debt

Ir£ million

	1982	1983	1984	1985	1986	1987	1988	1989	1990
Net borrowing[1]									
Government	2 464	2 216	2 265	2 239	2 334	1 955	627	445	838
Semi-state bodies	1 945	1 756	1 825	2 015	2 145	1 786	619	479	462
	519	460	440	224	189	169	8	−34	376
Outstanding debt (year-end)									
Government[2]	13 959	17 959	20 851	22 735	26 129	28 473	29 399	29 655	30 243
Semi-state bodies	11 669	14 392	16 821	18 502	21 611	23 691	24 610	24 828	25 110
	2 290	3 567	4 030	4 233	4 518	4 782	4 789	4 827	5 133
Interest payments									
Government[3]	1 249	1 456	1 705	1 967	1 989	2 118	2 141	2 141	2 300
Semi-state bodies		359	407	463	506	422	381	397	435

1. Includes net borrowing for capital and current purposes by the Government and by the Semi-state bodies and Local Authorities.
2. National Debt Statistics from 1982 onwards have been revised as a result of the enactment of the Local Loans Fund (Amendment) Act, 1987 which eliminates circular transfers.
3. Including sinking funds and expenses of issue.
Source: Department of Finance and Central Bank of Ireland, *Quarterly Bulletin.*

Table J. **Public sector external debt**[1]

Ir£ million

	1982	1983	1984	1985	1986	1987	1988	1989	1990
Gross external borrowing	2 045	1 515	1 533	1 285	1 443	1 073	-82	463	733
Government	1 589	1 167	1 322[2]	1 098[3]	1 148[4]	1 005[5]	-166[6]	150[7]	342[8]
Semi-state bodies	436	348	306	127	295	68	84	313	391
Net external borrowing	1 461	951	755	753	917	475	-674	51	194
Government	1 148	793	649	806	812	592	-443	-29	-44
Semi-state bodies	313	158	106	-53	105	-117	-231	80	238
Outstanding external debt (year-end)	6 917	8 931	10 075	10 060	11 513	11 961	11 534	11 231	11 120
Government	5 248	6 899	7 910	8 114	9 220	9 690	9 495	9 123	8 852
Semi-state bodies	1 669	2 032	2 165	1 946	2 293	2 271	2 039	2 109	2 268
Interest payments	650	748	885	987	940	884	869	906	918
Government	516	579	702	783	716	722	703	736	730
Semi-state bodies	134	169	183	204	224	162	166	170	188
Memorandum:									
Official external (year-end) reserves	1 594	2 015	2 101	2 272	2 205	2 821	3 161	2 521	2 892
Net external liability of licensed banks	2 077	2 806	3 237	3 361	3 821	3 578	3 928	3 584	4 056
Net external banking assets(+)/liabilities(-)	-483	-791	-1 136	-1 089	-1 616	-757	-767	-1 063	-1 166
Foreign holdings of Irish Government securities:									
Net Sales (+ denotes nonresident purchases)[9]	-18	+35	+121	+83	+240	+460	+867	+1 320	+64
Outstanding[10]	376	412	529	890	1 176	1 800	2 690	3 829	3 892

1. Excludes foreign holdings of Irish Government Securities which are shown separately in the Memorandum items.
2. Excluding prepayments and renegotiations of £831m.
3. Excluding prepayments and renegotiations of £1 222m.
4. Excluding prepayments and renegotiations of £1 239m.
5. Excluding prepayments and renegotiations of £946m.
6. Excluding prepayments and renegotiations of £726m.
7. Excluding prepayments and renegotiations of £529m.
8. Excluding prepayments and renegotiations of £499m.
9. Gilts and Exchequer bills.
10. Figures prior to 1984 refer to gilts only. From 1984 figures refer to gilts and exchequer bills.
*Sources:*Department of Finance and Central Bank.

Table K. Balance of payments

OECD basis; US$ million

	1979	1980	1981	1982	1983	1984	1985	1986	1987	1988	1989
Exports, fob	6 951	8 254	7 738	7 949	8 499	9 453	10 154	12 324	15 544	18 410	20 353
Imports, fob	9 273	10 482	9 978	9 076	8 710	9 203	9 527	11 184	12 941	14 575	16 337
Trade balance	-2 322	-2 228	-2 239	-1 127	-211	250	627	1 140	2 603	3 836	4 016
Services, net	-925	-1 119	-1 191	-1 606	-1 786	-2 086	-2 362	-3 109	-3 555	-4 711	-5 061
Balance on goods and services	-3 247	-3 347	-3 430	-2 733	-1 997	-1 836	-1 735	-1 969	-952	-876	-1 044
Private transfers, net	92	126	97	91	57	-34	-20	-57	-161	-120	-93
Official transfers, net	1 052	1 086	756	757	786	843	1 062	1 343	1 469	1 662	1 663
Current balance	-2 103	-2 135	-2 577	-1 885	-1 154	-1 027	-694	-684	356	666	526
Long-term capital (excluding special transactions)	1 294	1 496	2 322	2 095	982	766	988	1 067	853	-347	-1 212
a) Private[1]	536	369	386	360	92	-163	-109	-542	-980	-1 145	-2 582
b) Official	758	1 127	1 936	1 735	889	930	1 097	1 609	1 832	798	1 370
Basic balance	-809	-639	-255	210	-172	-261	294	383	1 208	320	-686
Non-monetary short-term official capital	-4	2	-2	-1	0	-2	-1	0	0	0	-4
Errors and omissions	-156	122	186	-330	-316	-187	-385	-1 219	-94	-225	116
Balance on non-monetary transactions	-968	-515	-71	-121	-488	-450	-92	-836	1 114	95	-574
Private monetary institutions' short-term capital	383	1 232	82	234	771	413	298	739	-213	442	-333
Balance on official settlements	-586	717	11	114	283	-37	207	-97	901	537	-907
Use of IMF credit, special transactions + other	–	–	–	–	–	–	–	–	–	–	–
Allocation of SDRs	20	21	18	–	–	–	–	–	–	–	–
Change in reserves (+ = increase)	-565	738	29	114	283	-37	207	-97	901	537	-907
a) Gold	-4	0	110	-7	31	-5	-13	-1	11	-12	-8
b) Currency assets	-592	713	-100	131	217	-65	236	-122	872	534	-902
c) Reserve positions in IMF	2	21	-2	0	45	9	-4	12	0	5	-12
d) Special drawing rights	31	–	23	6	-10	26	-10	15	17	11	14

1. Includes non-monetary short-term private capital.
Source: Direct communication to the OECD.

Table L. **Foreign trade and payments**

	1981	1982	1983	1984	1985	1986	1987	1988	1989	1990
Imports, Ir£ million	6 578.4	6 816.2	7 366.8	8 912.2	9 428.2	8 621.3	9 155.2	10 214.8	12 287.8	12 472.1
Exports Ir£ million	4 777.6	5 691.4	6 943.8	8 897.5	9 743.0	9 374.3	10 723.5	12 304.8	14 596.9	14 336.1
Trade balance Ir£ million	–1 800.8	–1 124.8	–423.0	–14.7	314.8	753.0	1 568.3	2 090.1	2 309.1	1 864.0
Volume of imports (1985=100)	87.9	84.9	87.6	96.8	100.0	100.3	109.4	114.5	129.3	138.5
Volume of exports (1985=100)	65.4	70.8	79.3	93.9	100.0	104.0	118.8	127.1	141.4	152.6
Import unit values (1985=100)	79.3	85.1	89.1	97.7	100.0	88.8	88.8	94.6	100.7	95.5
Export unit values (1985=100)	74.3	82.5	89.8	97.3	100.0	92.7	92.7	99.3	105.9	96.5
Terms of trade	93.7	96.9	100.8	99.6	100.0	104.3	104.4	105.0	105.1	101.2
Official external reserves,[1]Ir£ million	1 473.1	1 594.0	2 014.8	2 101.2	2 271.9	2 205.3	2 821.4	3 161.0	2 521.0	2 891.7
"Swaps" liabilities, Ir£ million	60.0	195.0	50.0	50.0	105.0	577.0	40.0	0.0	0.0	–
Reserves net of "swaps", as % of imports	21.5	20.5	26.7	23.0	23.0	18.0	30.4	30.9	20.5	–

1. At end of year.

Sources: CSO, *Statistical Bulletin*; Central Bank of Ireland *Quarterly Bulletin*.

Table M. Foreign trade by commodities

$ million

	1983	1984	1985	1986	1987	1988	1989	1990[1]
					Exports, fob			
SITC Section								
0. Food and live animals	2 164.3	2 236.3	2 353.9	2 946.5	3 986.1	4 411.8	4 543.7	4 742.7
1. Beverages and tobacco	226.4	225.5	252.3	306.5	352.6	382.8	422.2	541.8
2. Crude materials, inedible, except fuels	353.1	522.8	455.7	522.1	629.5	802.1	853.9	856.2
3. Mineral fuels, lubricants and related materials	98.7	115.8	132.0	98.5	115.0	102.7	103.0	146.0
4. Animal and vegetable oils and fats	11.0	15.2	17.0	14.0	15.3	17.5	18.0	18.5
5. Chemicals	1 196.2	1 295.1	1 459.6	1 641.1	1 909.5	2 434.8	2 932.4	3 770.6
6. Manufactured goods, classified by materials	900.7	912.9	963.6	1 186.4	1 400.1	1 589.9	1 638.0	1 909.7
7. Machinery and transport equipment	2 252.1	2 763.0	3 084.5	3 840.9	5 011.3	5 845.8	6 593.4	7 444.2
8. Miscellaneous manufactured articles	1 032.5	1 074.0	1 153.4	1 489.0	1 942.6	2 439.1	2 778.4	3 378.8
9. Commodities and transactions not classified elsewhere	373.6	477.6	527.3	558.8	608.3	709.7	802.1	967.8
Total	8 608.5	9 638.1	10 399.2	12 603.7	15 970.5	18 736.1	20 685.1	23 776.5
					Imports, cif			
0. Food and live animals	1 054.2	1 014.8	1 060.3	1 317.6	1 466.2	1 624.8	1 636.3	1 856.7
1. Beverages and tobacco	90.7	92.4	110.8	129.7	155.3	191.8	197.7	255.6
2. Crude materials, inedible, except fuels	275.9	320.4	316.4	337.1	382.9	429.3	466.6	562.5
3. Mineral fuels, lubricants and related materials	1 238.6	1 203.9	1 196.3	982.5	1 006.5	869.7	963.5	1 332.7
4. Animal and vegetable oils and fats	42.0	59.3	62.7	55.2	56.0	66.1	68.9	66.8
5. Chemicals	1 046.0	1 122.5	1 176.3	1 404.8	1 675.7	1 958.2	2 148.7	2 576.2
6. Manufactured goods, classified by materials	1 462.4	1 489.9	1 508.8	1 836.7	2 146.6	2 528.1	2 652.7	3 192.3
7. Machinery and transport equipment	2 644.1	3 022.4	3 140.9	3 638.3	4 560.7	5 357.0	6 591.3	7 425.2
8. Miscellaneous manufactured articles	1 113.3	1 122.3	1 162.7	1 503.4	1 744.9	2 046.5	2 197.5	2 824.2
9. Commodities and transactions not classified elsewhere	201.9	243.4	313.6	358.4	418.7	486.1	492.3	592.8
Total	9 169.0	9 691.4	10 048.9	11 563.7	13 613.5	15 557.8	17 415.6	20 685.0

1. Provisional figures for 1990.

Sources: OECD, Foreign Trade Statistics.

133

STRUCTURAL ANNEX

Table N. Production structure and performance indicators

		Per cent share of GDP at factor cost		
		1970	1980	1989
A.	**Production structure**			
	Agriculture, forestry and fishing	16.9	11.6	11.0
	Industry	36.2	37.3	37.0
	Distribution, transport and communication	19.0	17.7	17.6
	Public administration and defence	5.8	6.8	5.9
	Other domestic	24.6	31.2	33.5
	Adjustment for financial services	−2.5	−4.5	−5.1

	Per cent share of total employment		
	1971	1980	1988
Agriculture, forestry and fishing	26.2	18.3	15.4
Mining and quarrying	1.0	1.0	0.6
Manufacturing	20.4	21.3	19.2
Electricity, gas and water	1.3	1.2	1.3
Construction	8.1	9.0	6.7
Services	43.0	49.2	56.9
Of which:			
Transport, storage and communication	5.8	6.1	5.9
Wholesale and retail trade	16.5	16.4	17.9
Finance, insurance and real estate	3.5	5.7	7.8
Community, social and personal services	17.0	20.2	24.9

	1971	1981	1988
B. **Other indicators**			
Sectoral composition of fixed asset investment by overseas companies (per cent):			
Manufacturing	–	–	95.1
Of which:			
Metals and engineering	–	–	28.6
Chemicals	–	–	25.2
Textile	–	–	12.0
Food	–	–	11.8
Non-manufacturing	–	–	4.9
R&D as percentage of GDP	0.78	0.78	0.86
Of which:			
Government	0.37	0.41	0.33

Sources: CSO, National Income and Expenditure; IDA (IDA regions only, grant aided investment only)]; OECD, Labour Statistics.

Table O. **Public sector**

		1960	1970	1980	1988
A.	**Budget indicators: general government accounts** (per cent of GDP)[1]				
	Current receipts	26.9	34.7	38.8	44.9
	Non-interest expenditure	24.0	29.6	38.5	39.0
	Primary budget balance	2.9	5.1	0.3	5.9
	Net interest payments	2.8	4.0	6.6	9.4
	General government budget balance	0.1	1.1	−6.3	−3.5
	Of which:				
	Central	–	1.4	−5.3	−3.0
	Local authorities	–	−0.4	−1.1	−0.4
	Social security	–	0.1	0.1	−0.1
	General government debt (net, per cent of GDP)	67.7	68.3	84.4	114.6
B.	**The structure of expenditure and taxation** (per cent of GDP)				
	General government expenditure	29.1	40.0	52.9	51.9
	Current consumption	13.0	15.3	20.9	18.4
	Transfers to persons	6.3	9.0	12.9	16.5
	Subsidies	3.2	4.8	3.8	4.2
	Net interest payments	2.8	4.0	6.6	9.4
	Capital formation	2.8	4.3	5.9	2.1
	General government expenditure by function				
	Education	–	5.1	6.0	5.7
	Transportation	–	3.4	4.7	2.1
	Health	–	4.5	8.0	6.0
	Pensions				
	Total tax revenue	22.6	30.9	34.4	41.2
	Income tax	4.7	8.9	12.6	16.8
	Of which:				
	Personal	3.8	6.2	11.0	15.1
	Social security	1.0	2.7	1.5	1.7
	Social security	1.1	2.5	4.9	5.7
	Consumption tax	15.6	19.1	16.8	18.5
	Tax rates (per cent)				
	Top rate of income tax	35[2]	35[2]	60	58
	Lower rate of income tax	–	–	25	35
	Corporate tax rate (full rate)	–	5[3]	45	47
	Consumption tax rate (standard rate)	–	25[4]	25	25

1. National accounts basis.
2. Standard rate. A variable surtax was also applied.
3. Turnover tax.
4. Wholesale tax.
Sources: Department of Finance, OECD Revenue Statistics.

Table P. **Labour market indicators**

	Cyclical Peak 1984	Cyclical Trough 1986	1985	1989
A. Labour market performance				
Standardised unemployment rate	15.4	17.1	16.8	15.0
Unemployment rate				
(Live Register): Total	16.4	18.1	17.7	17.9
Male	17.3	18.9	18.8	17.9
Female	14.3	15.9	15.7	18.0
Youth[1]	18.7	21.6	20.2	20.1
Share of long-term unemployment in total unemployment[2]	39.8	44.1	41.9	44.5
	1971	1980	1985	1989
B. Structural or institutional characteristics				
Participation rate[3]: Total	64.0	62.3	61.5	60.3
Male	80.7	76.3	74.1	71.4
Female	27.9	29.3	30.4	34.9
Employment/population (15-64 years)	61.1	57.8	50.8	50.9
Average hours worked	–	41.3	41.1	41.5
Part-time work (as per cent of dependent employment)	–	–	8.1	7.8
Wage and salary employees (per cent of total employment)	–	76.3*	76.0	75.7
Non-wage labour costs[4] (as percentage of total compensation)	–	9.8	12.2	12.2
Government unemployment insurance replacement ratio[5]	–	31.9	29.7	24.0
	1971 / 1961	1979 / 1971	1989 / 1980	
Average percentage changes (annual rates)				
Labour force	0.0	1.3	0.4	
Employment: Total	0.0	1.3	0.4	
Agriculture	–3.3	–2.6	–2.7	
Industries	2.1	1.7	–2.1	
Services	1.0	2.6	0.8	
Of which: Public sector	0.7	1.4	0.1	

*   1981.
1.   People between 15 and 24 years as a percentage of the labour force of the same age group.
2.   People looking for a job since one year or more.
3.   Labour force as a percentage of relevant population group, aged between 15 and 64 years.
4.   Employers' contributions to social security and pension funds.
5.   Total unemployment compensation payments as proportion of wages and salaries.
Sources: Department of Finance, OECD, Quaterly Labour Force Statistics.

BASIC STATISTICS

BASIC STATISTICS:

INTERNATIONAL COMPARISONS

	Units	Reference period[1]	Australia		Austria		Belgium	
Population								
Total	Thousands	1988	16 538		7 596		9 879	
Inhabitants per sq.km	Number	1988	2		91		324	
Net average annual increase over previous 10 years	%	1987	1.4		0.0		0.0	
Employment								
Total civilian employment (TCE)[2]	Thousands	1988	7 366		3 310		3 660	(8
of which: Agriculture	% of TCE		5.9		8.1		2.7	
Industry	% of TCE		26.4		37.4		28.0	
Services	% of TCE		67.8		54.5		69.3	
Gross domestic product (GDP)								
At current prices and current exchange rates	Bill US $	1988	247.0		127.2		150.0	
Per capita	US $		14 937		16 748		15 180	
At current prices using current PPP's[3]	Bill US $	1988	221.3		94.8		124.5	
Per capita	US $		13 383		12 482		12 599	
Average annual volume growth over previous 5 years . . .	%	1988	4.5		2.2		2.2	
Gross fixed capital formation (GFCF)	% of GDP	1988	25.0		23.5		17.8	
of which: Machinery and equipment	% of GDP		12.1		9.9		8.0	
Residential construction	% of GDP		5.9		4.9		4.1	
Average annual volume growth over previous 5 years . . .	%	1988	6.1		3.8		5.4	
Gross saving ratio[4]	% of GDP	1988	22.4		25.2		19.3	
General government								
Current expenditure on goods and services	% of GDP	1988	17.4		18.4		15.3	
Current disbursements[5]	% of GDP	1988	32.0		45.8		49.0	
Current receipts	% of GDP	1988	34.3		46.8		44.3	
Net official development assistance	% of GNP	1988	0.41		0.21		0.44	
Indicators of living standards								
Private consumption per capita using current PPP's	US $	1988	7 703		6 952		7 951	
Passenger cars, per 1 000 inhabitants	Number	1988	497	(85)	370		349	
Telephones, per 1 000 inhabitants	Number	1985	540	(83)	460	(83)	414	(
Television sets, per 1 000 inhabitants	Number	1985	..		300	(81)	303	(
Doctors, per 1 000 inhabitants	Number	1985	..		1.7	(82)	2.8	(
Infant mortality, per 1 000 live births	Number	1985	9.2	(84)	11.0		9.4	
Wages and prices (average annual increase over previous 5 years)								
Wages (earnings or rates according to availability	%	1988	5.3		4.5		2.7	
Consumer prices	%	1988	7.1		2.8		3.0	
Foreign trade								
Exports of goods, fob*	Mill US $	1988	32 852		31 044		92 124[7]	
As % of GDP	%		13.3		24.4		58.8	
Average annual increase over previous 5 years	%		10.3		15.0		12.1	
Imports of goods, cif*	Mill US $	1988	33 276		36 564		92 436[7]	
As % of GDP	%		13.4		28.7		59.0	
Average annual increase over previous 5 years	%		12.4		13.5		10.8	
Total official reserves[6]	Mill SDR's	1988	10 105		5 475		6 935[7]	
As ratio of average monthly imports of goods	ratio		3.6		1.8		0.9	

(*) At current prices and exchange rates.
1. Unless otherwise stated.
2. According to the definitions used in OECD Labour Force Statistics.
3. PPP's=Purchasing Power Parities.
4. Gross saving = Gross national disposable income minus Private and Government consumption.
5. Current disbursements = Current expenditure on goods and services plus current transfers and payments of property income.
6. Gold included in reserves is valued at 35 SDR's per ounce. End of year.

EMPLOYMENT OPPORTUNITIES
Economics and Statistics Department, OECD

The Economics and Statistics Department of the OECD offers challenging and rewarding opportunities to economists interested in applied policy analysis in an international environment. The Department's concerns extend across the entire field of economic policy analysis, both macroeconomic and microeconomic, and it is also responsible for the collection, processing and dissemination of a wide range of internationally consistent statistics. On the economic side, its main task is to provide, for discussion by committees of senior officials from Member countries, documents and papers dealing with current policy concerns. Within this programme of work, three major responsibilities are:

- To prepare regular surveys of the economies of individual Member countries;
- To issue full twice-yearly reviews of the economic situation and prospects of the OECD countries in the context of world economic trends;
- To analyse specific policy issues in a medium-term context for the OECD as a whole, and to a lesser extent for the non-OECD countries.

The documents prepared for these purposes, together with much of the Department's other economic work and its statistical output, appear in published form in the *OECD Economic Outlook, OECD Economic Surveys, OECD Economic Studies,* the Department's *Working Papers* series, and an extensive list of statistical publications.

The Department maintains a world econometric model, INTERLINK, which plays an important role in the preparation of the policy analyses and twice-yearly projections. The availability of extensive cross-country data bases and good computer resources facilitates comparative empirical analysis, much of which is incorporated into the model.

The Department is made up of about 100 professional economists and statisticians from a variety of backgrounds from all Member countries. Most projects are done by small teams and last from four to eighteen months. Within the Department, ideas and points of view are widely discussed; there is a lively professional interchange; and all professional staff have the opportunity to contribute actively to the programme of work.

Skills ESD is looking for:

a) Solid competence in using the tools of both microeconomic and macroeconomic theory to answer policy questions. In our experience this requires the equivalent of a PhD in economics or substantial relevant professional experience to compensate for a lower degree.

b) Solid knowledge of economic statistics and quantitative methods; this includes how to identify data, estimate structural relationships, apply and interpret basic techniques of time series analysis, and test hypotheses. It is essential to be able to interpret results sensibly in an economic policy context.

c) A keen interest in and knowledge of policy issues, economic developments and their political/social contexts.

d) Interest and experience in analysing questions posed by policy-makers and presenting the results to them effectively and judiciously. Thus, work experience in government agencies or policy research institutions is an advantage.

e) The ability to write clearly, effectively, and to the point. The OECD is a bilingual organisation with French and English as the official languages. Candidates must have excellent knowledge of one of these languages, and some knowledge of the other. Knowledge of other languages might also be an advantage for certain posts.

f) For some posts, expertise in a particular area may be important, but a successful candidate can expect to be asked to contribute in a broader range of topics relevant to the work of the Department. Thus, except in rare cases, the Department does not recruit narrow specialists.

g) The Department works on a tight time schedule and strict deadlines. Moreover, much of the work in the Department is carried out in small groups of economists. Thus, the ability to work with other economists from a variety of professional backgrounds, and to produce work on time is important.

General Information

The salary for recruits depends on educational and professional background but positions carry a basic salary from FF 252 888 or FF 312 036 for Administrators (economists) and from FF 363 012 for Principal Administrators (senior economists). This may be supplemented by expatriation and/or family allowances, depending on nationality, residence and family situation. Initial appointments are for a fixed term of two to three years.

Vacancies are open to candidates from OECD Member countries. The Organisation seeks to maintain an appropriate balance between female and male staff and among nationals from Member countries.

For further information on employment opportunities in the Economics and Statistics Department, contact:

Executive Assistant
Economics and Statistics Department
OECD
2, rue André-Pascal
75775 PARIS CEDEX 16
FRANCE

Applications citing "ECSUR", together with a detailed curriculum vitae in English or French, should be sent to:

Head of Personnel
OECD
2, rue André-Pascal
75775 PARIS CEDEX 16
FRANCE

WHERE TO OBTAIN OECD PUBLICATIONS – OÙ OBTENIR LES PUBLICATIONS DE L'OCDE

Argentina – Argentine
CARLOS HIRSCH S.R.L.
Galería Güemes, Florida 165, 4° Piso
1333 Buenos Aires   Tel. 30.7122, 331.1787 y 331.2391
Telegram: Hirsch-Baires
Telex: 21112 UAPE-AR. Ref. s/2901
Telefax:(1)331-1787

Australia – Australie
D.A. Book (Aust.) Pty. Ltd.
648 Whitehorse Road, P.O.B 163
Mitcham, Victoria 3132   Tel. (03)873.4411
Telex: AA37911 DA BOOK
Telefax: (03)873.5679

Austria – Autriche
OECD Publications and Information Centre
Schedestrasse 7
DW–5300 Bonn 1 (Germany)   Tel. (49.228)21.60.45
Telefax: (49.228)26.11.04
Gerold & Co.
Graben 31
Wien I   Tel. (0222)533.50.14

Belgium – Belgique
Jean De Lannoy
Avenue du Roi 202
B-1060 Bruxelles   Tel. (02)538.51.69/538.08.41
Telex: 63220   Telefax: (02) 538.08.41

Canada
Renouf Publishing Company Ltd.
1294 Algoma Road
Ottawa, ON K1B 3W8   Tel. (613)741.4333
Telex: 053-4783   Telefax: (613)741.5439
Stores:
61 Sparks Street
Ottawa, ON K1P 5R1   Tel. (613)238.8985
211 Yonge Street
Toronto, ON M5B 1M4   Tel. (416)363.3171
Federal Publications
165 University Avenue
Toronto, ON M5H 3B8   Tel. (416)581.1552
Telefax: (416)581.1743
Les Publications Fédérales
1185 rue de l'Université
Montréal, PQ H3B 3A7   Tel.(514)954-1633
Les Éditions La Liberté Inc.
3020 Chemin Sainte-Foy
Sainte-Foy, PQ G1X 3V6   Tel. (418)658.3763
Telefax: (418)658.3763

Denmark – Danemark
Munksgaard Export and Subscription Service
35, Nørre Søgade, P.O. Box 2148
DK-1016 København K   Tel. (45 33)12.85.70
Telex: 19431 MUNKS DK   Telefax: (45 33)12.93.87

Finland – Finlande
Akateeminen Kirjakauppa
Keskuskatu 1, P.O. Box 128
00100 Helsinki   Tel. (358 0)12141
Telex: 125080   Telefax: (358 0)121.4441

France
OECD/OCDE
Mail Orders/Commandes par correspondance:
2, rue André-Pascal
75775 Paris Cédex 16   Tel. (33-1)45.24.82.00
Bookshop/Librairie:
33, rue Octave-Feuillet
75016 Paris   Tel. (33-1)45.24.81.67
                            (33-1)45.24.81.81
Telex: 620 160 OCDE
Telefax: (33-1)45.24.85.00 (33-1)45.24.81.76
Librairie de l'Université
12a, rue Nazareth
13100 Aix-en-Provence   Tel. 42.26.18.08
Telefax : 42.26.63.26

Germany – Allemagne
OECD Publications and Information Centre
Schedestrasse 7
DW–5300 Bonn 1   Tel. (0228)21.60.45
Telefax: (0228)26.11.04

Greece – Grèce
Librairie Kauffmann
28 rue du Stade
105 64 Athens   Tel. 322.21.60
Telex: 218187 LIKA Gr

Hong Kong
Swindon Book Co. Ltd.
13 - 15 Lock Road
Kowloon, Hong Kong   Tel. 366.80.31
Telex: 50 441 SWIN HX   Telefax: 739.49.75

Iceland – Islande
Mál Mog Menning
Laugavegi 18, Pósthólf 392
121 Reykjavik   Tel. 15199/24240

India – Inde
Oxford Book and Stationery Co.
Scindia House
New Delhi 110001   Tel. 331.5896/5308
Telex: 31 61990 AM IN
Telefax: (11)332.5993
17 Park Street
Calcutta 700016   Tel. 240832

Indonesia – Indonésie
Pdii-Lipi
P.O. Box 269/JKSMG/88
Jakarta 12790   Tel. 583467
Telex: 62 875

Ireland – Irlande
TDC Publishers – Library Suppliers
12 North Frederick Street
Dublin 1   Tel. 744835/749677
Telex: 33530 TDCP EI   Telefax: 748416

Italy – Italie
Libreria Commissionaria Sansoni
Via Benedetto Fortini, 120/10
Casella Post. 552
50125 Firenze   Tel. (055)64.54.15
Telex: 570466   Telefax: (055)64.12.57
Via Bartolini 29
20155 Milano   Tel. 36.50.83
La diffusione delle pubblicazioni OCSE viene assicurata
dalle principali librerie ed anche da:
Editrice e Libreria Herder
Piazza Montecitorio 120
00186 Roma   Tel. 679.46.28
Telex: NATEL I 621427
Libreria Hoepli
Via Hoepli 5
20121 Milano   Tel. 86.54.46
Telex: 31.33.95   Telefax: (02)805.28.86
Libreria Scientifica
Dott. Lucio de Biasio 'Aeiou'
Via Meravigli 16
20123 Milano   Tel. 805.68.98
Telefax: 800175

Japan – Japon
OECD Publications and Information Centre
Landic Akasaka Building
2-3-4 Akasaka, Minato-ku
Tokyo 107   Tel. (81.3)3586.2016
Telefax: (81.3)3584.7929

Korea – Corée
Kyobo Book Centre Co. Ltd.
P.O. Box 1658, Kwang Hwa Moon
Seoul   Tel. (REP)730.78.91
Telefax: 735.0030

Malaysia/Singapore – Malaisie/Singapour
Co-operative Bookshop Ltd.
University of Malaya
P.O. Box 1127, Jalan Pantai Baru
59700 Kuala Lumpur
Malaysia   Tel. 756.5000/756.5425
Telefax: 757.3661
Information Publications Pte. Ltd.
Pei-Fu Industrial Building
24 New Industrial Road No. 02-06
Singapore 1953   Tel. 283.1786/283.1798
Telefax: 284.8875

Netherlands – Pays-Bas
SDU Uitgeverij
Christoffel Plantijnstraat 2
Postbus 20014
2500 EA's-Gravenhage   Tel. (070 3)78.99.11
Voor bestellingen: Tel. (070 3)78.98.80
Telex: 32486 stdru   Telefax: (070 3)47.63.51

New Zealand – Nouvelle-Zélande
GP Publications Ltd.
Customer Services
33 The Esplanade - P.O. Box 38-900
Petone, Wellington
Tel. (04)685-555   Telefax: (04)685-333

Norway – Norvège
Narvesen Info Center - NIC
Bertrand Narvesens vei 2
P.O. Box 6125 Etterstad
0602 Oslo 6   Tel. (02)57.33.00
Telex: 79668 NIC N   Telefax: (02)68.19.01

Pakistan
Mirza Book Agency
65 Shahrah Quaid-E-Azam
Lahore 3   Tel. 66839
Telex: 44886 UBL PK. Attn: MIRZA BK

Portugal
Livraria Portugal
Rua do Carmo 70-74
Apart. 2681
1117 Lisboa Codex   Tel.: 347.49.82/3/4/5
Telefax: (01) 347.02.64

Singapore/Malaysia – Singapour/Malaisie
See Malaysia/Singapore" – Voir «Malaisie/Singapour»

Spain – Espagne
Mundi-Prensa Libros S.A.
Castelló 37, Apartado 1223
Madrid 28001   Tel. (91) 431.33.99
Telex: 49370 MPLI   Telefax: 575.39.98
Libreria Internacional AEDOS
Consejo de Ciento 391
08009-Barcelona   Tel. (93) 301.86.15
Telefax: (93) 317.01.41

Sri Lanka
Centre for Policy Research
c/o Mercantile Credit Ltd.
55, Janadhipathi Mawatha
Colombo 1   Tel. 438471-9, 440346
Telex: 21138 VAVALEX CE   Telefax: 94.1.448900

Sweden – Suède
Fritzes Fackboksföretaget
Box 16356, S 103 27 STH
Regeringsgatan 12
DS Stockholm   Tel. (08)23.89.00
Telex: 12387   Telefax: (08)20.50.21
Subscription Agency/Abonnements:
Wennergren-Williams AB
Nordenflychtsvagen 74
Box 30004
104 25 Stockholm   Tel. (08)13.67.00
Telex: 19937   Telefax: (08)618.62.36

Switzerland – Suisse
OECD Publications and Information Centre
Schedestrasse 7
DW–5300 Bonn 1 (Germany)   Tel. (49.228)21.60.45
Telefax: (49.228)26.11.04
Librairie Payot
6 rue Grenus
1211 Genève 11   Tel. (022)731.89.50
Telex: 28356
Subscription Agency – Service des Abonnements
Naville S.A.
7, rue Lévrier
1201 Genève   Tél.: (022) 732.24.00
Telefax: (022) 738.48.03
Maditec S.A.
Chemin des Palettes 4
1020 Renens/Lausanne   Tel. (021)635.08.65
Telefax: (021)635.07.80
United Nations Bookshop/Librairie des Nations-Unies
Palais des Nations
1211 Genève 10   Tel. (022)734.60.11 (ext. 48.72)
Telex: 289696 (Attn: Sales)   Telefax: (022)733.98.79

Taiwan – Formose
Good Faith Worldwide Int'l. Co. Ltd.
9th Floor, No. 118, Sec. 2
Chung Hsiao E. Road
Taipei   Tel. 391.7396/391.7397
Telefax: (02) 394.9176

Thailand – Thaïlande
Suksit Siam Co. Ltd.
1715 Rama IV Road, Samyan
Bangkok 5   Tel. 251.1630

Turkey – Turquie
Kültur Yayinlari Is-Türk Ltd. Sti.
Atatürk Bulvari No. 191/Kat. 21
Kavaklidere/Ankara   Tel. 25.07.60
Dolmabahce Cad. No. 29
Besiktas/Istanbul   Tel. 160.71.88
Telex: 43482B

United Kingdom – Royaume-Uni
HMSO
Gen. enquiries   Tel. (071) 873 0011
Postal orders only:
P.O. Box 276, London SW8 5DT
Personal Callers HMSO Bookshop
49 High Holborn, London WC1V 6HB
Telex: 297138   Telefax: 071 873 8463
Branches at: Belfast, Birmingham, Bristol, Edinburgh,
Manchester

United States – États-Unis
OECD Publications and Information Centre
2001 L Street N.W., Suite 700
Washington, D.C. 20036-4095   Tel. (202)785.6323
Telefax: (202)785.0350

Venezuela
Libreria del Este
Avda F. Miranda 52, Aptdo. 60337
Edificio Galipán
Caracas 106   Tel. 951.1705/951.2307/951.1297
Telegram: Libreste Caracas

Yugoslavia – Yougoslavie
Jugoslovenska Knjiga
Knez Mihajlova 2, P.O. Box 36
Beograd   Tel.: (011)621.992
Telex: 12466 jk bgd   Telefax: (011)625.970

Orders and inquiries from countries where Distributors
have not yet been appointed should be sent to: OECD
Publications Service, 2 rue André-Pascal, 75775 Paris
Cedex 16, France.

Les commandes provenant de pays où l'OCDE n'a pas
encore désigné de distributeur devraient être adressées à :
OCDE, Service des Publications, 2, rue André-Pascal,
75775 Paris Cédex 16, France.

75490–1/91

PRINTED IN FRANCE

●

OECD PUBLICATIONS
2 rue André-Pascal
75775 PARIS CEDEX 16
No. 45575
(10 91 18 1) ISBN 92-64-13492-1
ISSN 0376-6438

●